THE EUCHARIST
WHAT DO WE BELIEVE?

To the Redemptorist Community in Marianella, Rathgar,
with thanks for their friendship and Eucharistic hospitality
over many years.

Greatly appreciated, and formative.

Fáinche Ryan

The Eucharist
What do we believe?

the columba press

First published in 2012 by
the columba press
55A Spruce Avenue, Stillorgan Industrial Park,
Blackrock, Co Dublin

Cover by Bill Bolger
Origination by The Columba Press
Printed by the MPG Books Group

ISBN 978-1-85607-7880

Scripture quotations are taken from the New Revised Standard Version,
copyright © 1989, by the Division of Christian Education of the National
Council of Churches of Christ in the United States of America

Contents

Acknowledgements

At a meeting with some parents of first communion children, one of the parents told me of his daughter's question, a child preparing for first communion, coming home from school and asking if she could put jam on the 'Holy Bread'. He himself professed that he was somewhat at a loss to respond, easy to say no, but then 'Why not?', don't bread and jam go well together? This question struck me and reminded me of how difficult it is to get good solid information on the Catholic Church, of the problem of knowing where to go to get answers to our questions.

This book will try to help that parent explain to his child why it is not a good idea to put jam on Holy Communion, and also invite him to wonder why Catholics do what they do, and what is understood by the 'Eucharist'. The content and structure of the book has been influenced by the many questions put to me from encounters with members of parishes, parents of first communicants, friends who have drifted from their faith, those curious and who might be considering taking the awesome step of baptism, and not least questions from those actively involved in Church ministry. For this stimulation I am intensely grateful.

Thanks is also due to those who read earlier drafts of this work and offered helpful critique – Brendan McConvery, Tom Whelan, Ethna Regan and Joe Egan.

CHAPTER ONE

On being Catholic
'Abide in me' (Jn 15:4)

One problem with being a Catholic in Ireland today is that in one sense we know too much, but in another we know very little. We know there are certain things that Catholics do, and we do them, or at least we did them religiously in the past. Many of us were never too sure why we did them, and often it is when our children are born that we begin to wonder should we baptise them. Is there any reason for them to make their first communion other than to have a great family day out, expensive though it might be. This book will seek to explain what it means to be a Catholic, to be a member of a Church in which to celebrate something called the Eucharist is central. It will try to inform you, the reader, so you can better understand what it is to be a Catholic, or decide if you would like to bring up your children as Catholics, depending on where you are coming from.

The Church, the People of God
A famous French theologian, Henri de Lubac, once said that 'the Church makes the Eucharist' and 'the Eucharist makes the Church'. In other words, the two are intimately connected, and so if we are to discuss the Eucharist we need to begin by thinking about the word 'Church' and wondering what it means, or what we understand by it. Very often we think of the Church as the building that we went to as children, that we loved going to and have lovely memories of, or alternately, as a place we dreaded going to, a place of boredom and cold. Whatever our memories they tend to simply refer to the church building, a physical construction built by humans. Similarly today many understand the word Church as referring solely to the men in Rome, primarily the Pope, and also maybe our own bishop and the priest(s) in our parish. Once again this is a man-made understanding of Church, seeing it solely in institutional terms, and,

while very much part of the story, to understand the Church like this is to limit the idea of Church too much.

The Second Vatican Council (1962 – 1965) devoted a lot of time to the task of discovering how best we might understand what it means to be Church, to be a member of the community that follows Jesus Christ. Looking back over our tradition, and in particular at the early days, the years after the resurrection of Jesus, the teachings of the Second Vatican Council suggested that the Church is best understood as the People of God, all the baptised, equal in the eyes of God. Indeed it is a human structure, composed of human beings, both sinful and holy, and yet we believe in the presence of the Holy Spirit, present and active in the Church, among the people and hopefully guiding us. The Church is thus best understood as a community of all the baptised, guided by the Holy Spirit, trying to live in the world as Christians. We often say it is both a human institution and a divine mystery. In other words, because it is a human institution it is made up of fallible, fragile human beings and so often makes mistakes, but it is at once a divine mystery with God present guiding us gently. For this reason we believe, in faith, that the Church will always have holy people in it, and that it will ultimately be a source of goodness. We believe that it helps people to both live well in this life and to journey through death to life everlasting with God. This is our faith.

A key point to remember is that the Church in its current form was not always this way. Indeed we often seem to forget that Jesus the Christ was a Jew, and died a Jew crucified on a cross. What is remarkable is that this person who died on a cross was resurrected from the dead – 'God raised him on the third day and allowed him to appear' (Acts 10:40). This came as a big shock to his followers, and they found it hard to believe, but slowly they came to understand what was going on. The death and resurrection of Jesus Christ are central to the Christian faith, one could say they are the foundation events of the Church. This is the story which 'makes' Christians, the story which we retell over and over again as we seek to learn, at a deeper level, what it means to be a Christian. It is important to remember that we are Christian first, Christians who express our faith through the traditions of the Catholic Church.[1]

God is Love

To be a Christian means quite simply to be a follower of Christ. In the Acts of the Apostles we read that 'it was in Antioch that the disciples were first called "Christians"' (Acts 11:26). To be a Christian is to be a follower of Christ, it is an invitation to live differently, to radically reorient our values and to try to live lives which accord with the values by which Jesus lived. To be a Christian is to always seek to learn more about the God whom Jesus taught us to call 'Our Father'. To be a Christian is to be a member of a community, a community called Church. The Church, founded by Jesus, progressed by people who believed Jesus had an important message to proclaim, that of God's saving presence in human history, a presence which became manifest in a particular way in the life of Jesus. These people, the early Christians, wished to tell this story, and to proclaim to the whole world the fact that the Holy Spirit has been gifted to us, promising newness of life. The Holy Spirit both invites and empowers us to live differently, to seek to live and die as Jesus did.

It is, however, difficult to live as Jesus lived, and virtually impossible alone. For this reason, from the earliest days Christians have gathered together: to pray together, to worship the God that is Trinity, and then to go back to their everyday life to proclaim this God of love to others. Love has always been central to the Christian journey, 'By this everyone will know that you are my disciples, if you have love for one another' (Jn 13:35), and this should come to us as no surprise because Love is a name for God – as we read in the first letter of John, 'God is love' (1 Jn 4:16).

Pope Benedict XVI chose to name his first major writing as Pope (Bishop of Rome) *Deus Caritas Est*, after this passage from scripture. The opening paragraphs of this encyclical give a summary of the Christian vocation:

> 'God is love, and he who abides in love abides in God, and God abides in him' (1 Jn 4:16). These words from the First Letter of John express with remarkable clarity the heart of the Christian faith: the Christian image of God and the resulting image of humankind and its destiny. In the same verse, Saint John also offers a kind of summary

of the Christian life: 'We have come to know and to believe in the love God has for us.'

These words express the fundamental principal of a Christian life: a Christian is someone who has come to know and to believe in God's love. This can only come through an encounter with the living God, a God who is love, an encounter which gives life new meaning, and gives new direction to all that one does. An encounter which invites a response, a changed way of living, and an encounter which teaches that life does not end with death. The centrality of love is a message we have inherited from our Jewish brothers and sisters, something they acknowledge every time they pray the *Shema*: 'Hear, O Israel: The Lord is our God, the Lord alone. You shall love the Lord your God with all your heart, and with all your soul, and with all your might' (Deut 6:4-5).[2] Benedict XVI goes on to remind Christians that 'Since God has first loved us (cf. 1 Jn 4:10), love is no longer a mere "command"; it is the response to the gift of love with which God draws near to us.'

Sacrament

This gift of love, for Christians, is primarily named as Jesus the Christ, the Son of God. In a sense Jesus is love incarnate, love visible in human flesh. It is the story of Jesus Christ, which forms Christians into a people. From the early days of the Christian community one became an identifiable member of the community through the ceremony called baptism. One of our earliest accounts of this is in an ancient document called the *Didache* which speaks of baptising people with water and in the name of the Trinity.[3] Today it remains the case that most Christian Churches mark entry into their community by baptism with water and in the name of the Trinity. Once baptised a person could then participate fully in eucharistic gatherings, and eat at the eucharistic table. While a person is 'made' a Christian when baptised, one spends the rest of one's life really 'becoming' a Christian through prayer and regular celebration of the Eucharist. Gathering to celebrate the Eucharist has been the mark of a Christian from the very earliest days. The Eucharist has always been the place where Christians gathered to hear again the story of the life, death and resurrection of Jesus, and by hearing the story becoming more and more transformed into the story.

Most Christian Churches baptise and celebrate the Eucharist, although we may use different names and we may have different understandings of what we do. In their liturgies Christians remember the great love of God in sending his Son to live among us, and in raising him from the dead after his crucifixion.

The Catholic Church calls baptism and Eucharist sacraments. It also identifies five other key moments in the Catholic life as sacraments – confirmation, reconciliation, marriage, ordination and the sacrament of the sick. What all these events have in common is that they are key moments of encounter with the Divine, if you like 'concentrated' meetings with God. While the Church very firmly believes in God's presence everywhere, that there is no place in this world from which God is absent, it is often hard to remember this. The sacraments serve to remind us of this; God is with us, always ('Do not fear, for I am with you, do not be afraid, for I am your God', [Is 41: 10]).

But what precisely are sacraments? Are they some form of magic? To an outsider viewing a baptism, a Eucharist or any of the sacraments, they must seem very strange. And where did they come from? Christ of course, for Christ is the sacrament of God. In Christ, God's words of grace, of mercy and of salvation are made visible. So while we did not have seven sacraments from the time of Jesus, the Catechism teaches that,

> the Church, by the power of the Spirit who guides her 'into all truth', has gradually recognized this treasure received from Christ … the Church has discerned over the centuries that among liturgical celebrations there are seven that are, in the strict sense of the term, sacraments instituted by the Lord (*Catechism of the Catholic Church*, n. 1117).

These seven are sacraments of the Church, making people holy, forming a priestly people, bringing us into communion with God, and even more spectacularly, as we shall see when we come to discuss the Eucharist, deifying us, making us 'like unto God'.[4] Sacraments are transformative, effecting that which they signify. The document on the liturgy from Vatican II expresses what Catholics understand by sacraments most beautifully:

> The purpose of the sacraments is to sanctify people, to build up the Body of Christ and, finally, to give worship to God. Because they are signs they also instruct. They not only presuppose faith, but by words and objects they also nourish, strengthen and express it. That is why they are called 'sacraments of faith' (*Sacrosanctum Concilium* 59).[5]

Sacraments are signs of God. We use bread, wine, water and oil and we speak of these things as signs of God. Matter, earthly matter, speaks to us of God. This is so because, if we recall the story of Creation in Genesis we read that God saw 'all that God had made and indeed it was very good' (Gen 1:31). This is the message of Christianity – creation is good. The truth of this fact, and indeed the regard with which God beholds humanity is particularly emphasised in the incarnation, the wonderful gift to us of the Word which became flesh. God deigned to take on our humanity, human flesh, in this way ensuring that forever we will remember that we are good, body and spirit. With the incarnation God revealed to us how we might be, what we might become, as humans, created after God's image and likeness. In every sacrament we celebrate we remember this and we give thanks for the goodness of all of creation, especially for the gift of our humanity, a nature gifted with a reason, a mind, which enables us to consciously give thanks to God.

Words, as well as objects, are central to sacraments. Remembering that in our sacraments God is acting, we might say that our words become God's words, our language God's language. We encounter, at a most profound level, Jesus Christ, the Word of God. In each sacrament celebrated we enter into the story of Jesus Christ, the story of a life, a death on a cross and a resurrection into eternal life. Sacraments are God in action, and they are simultaneously the human response to God, they are most profoundly an invitation to enter into the relationship between Jesus and the Father, and to allow the Holy Spirit to transform us and prepare us for life everlasting. Sacraments are efficacious, so the Church has always taught, they cause what they signify because in the sacraments it is Christ acting, Christ who is praying, and the Father always responds to the words of his Son. At the same time sacraments are sacraments of faith, so faith is necessary if the Holy Spirit is to transform us. The power of God is the power of love and gentleness, God's grace never forces itself, to be transformed we must wish to be transformed.

Making Holy
Before moving to look specifically at that most beautiful of all sacraments, the Eucharist, it is helpful to summarise what has been said thus far of sacraments. They are essentially encounters with the extraordinary through the ordinary. The seven sacraments are sacraments of the Church, celebrations of a priestly people, a people of faith. They are encounters with a God who claims to love us for ever, who will never reject us although we are always free to reject God. We can choose to become unloving; we are free to reject the goodness in which we have been created. The God whom we encounter is so awe-inspiring, described by one theologian as a *mysterium tremendum*, that were we to encounter this God 'face to face' we would be overcome at this rather terrifying and tremendous mystery that God became human. God became human and walked among us, now our invitation is to encounter God the Second Person of the Trinity, the one who became flesh and blood like us.

In each sacrament we enter into the story of Jesus – Jesus' life and even more profoundly his death and resurrection. Although we may receive the consecrated elements individually at the Eucharist, or go to the sacrament of reconciliation alone, all the sacraments are best understood as celebrations of a people, and so are best celebrated in that community called Church, and celebrated as a community. Sacraments are efficacious (effective) because through them God is acting, they are not dependent on the holiness of the person ministering the sacraments, God has always acted through frail and vulnerable human vessels. God acts in the sacraments forming a people into God's image and likeness. When a person is baptised they begin the story of their encounter with God in a visible way, they become visibly part of the Church community. Baptism, confirmation and ordination are sacraments that are received only once. The sacrament of reconciliation and the sacrament of the sick have come to be understood as sacraments of healing, and can be received more than once, whenever there is need. We have mentioned earlier the fact that sacraments are signs which also instruct, and the Eucharist is the sacrament where most of the instruction can take place. It really is the key sacrament involved in the making of a people, as it is celebrated so regularly, and recalls so clearly the story of Christ. Like all the sacraments it is forming us for life everlasting with God. St Thomas Aquinas (c.1225-1274), in his answer to the question, 'what is a sacrament?' very succinctly puts together all that this chapter has tried to say:

a sacrament properly speaking is that which is ordained to signify our sanctification. In which three things may be considered; the very cause of our sanctification, which is Christ's passion; the form of our sanctification, which is grace and the virtues; and the ultimate end of our sanctification, which is eternal life. And all these are signified by the sacraments. Consequently a sacrament is a sign that is both a reminder of the past, i.e. the passion of Christ; and an indication of that which is effected in us by Christ's passion, i.e. grace; and a prognostic, that is, a foretelling of future glory (*Summa Theologiae* III a.3 c).[6]

CHAPTER TWO

From Corinth to the Second Vatican Council
'Filled with the Holy Spirit' (Acts 2:4)

The last chapter ended with Thomas Aquinas' understanding of sacraments. Although he lived and wrote in the thirteenth century, what he said about sacraments remains true, and his teachings apply to the Eucharist in a very rich way. It really is a sacrament which speaks to us of Jesus' life, it reminds us of the great gift it is to be a Christian, and it promises us that we too shall enjoy glory, that even now we are enjoying a taste of the 'food' we shall feast on with God and all our loved ones in our life after death. As *Lumen Gentium* (*LG*), one of the documents of Vatican II, describes it, it really is 'the source and summit of Christian life' (*LG* 11), it is our 'daily bread'.[1] Some of us like to attend Mass to receive daily, some weekly, and some from time to time, maybe at the time of great feasts like Easter or Christmas, or for a funeral or a wedding. Whenever we come together for Eucharist we realise that we are doing something that Christians have been doing for generations, from the very earliest days of Christianity.

We fool ourselves, however, if we think that the way we do things now is the way that they were always done. Many Catholics who have memories of masses celebrated before the Second Vatican Council remember that what they did then was different in many ways from what we do now, and yet the essentials remain constant, the core of what we do has been stable since earliest times. But what is the core? Why do we do what we do? Some of us think we know a lot about these origins, but maybe we have a somewhat simplistic view of how it all began. Our idea of how it all began may be based on images passed on in tradition and history, images such as Leonardo da Vinci's famous painting of the Last Supper, where we have thirteen men sitting neatly around a table. Or we look to the

Bible, sacred scripture, for a literal historical account of what happened. However, any attempt to find out what happened is complex. History, an attempt to retell what happened in the past, is always influenced by surrounding culture and by the perspective of the person telling the story. The question this chapter seeks to address is how did we come to do what we do now? In answering this question we must first see what can be said about what Jesus and his disciples did, and then, perhaps more importantly, we must ask what was the human and religious meaning of what they did?

Jesus' Last Supper
One thing we are sure of is that Jesus shared a meal with his disciples the night before he was killed on a cross. There are accounts of this fact in Matthew, Mark and Luke (Mt 26:20-30; Mk 14:17-26; Lk 22:14-23) and in Paul's letter to the Corinthians (1 Cor 11:23-34). For Jewish people, this sharing of a meal with one's friends was an event rich in meaning, it was a real mark of fellowship whereby you identified yourself as part of the group with whom you ate, agreeing to live as they lived, abide by their customs. A meal was seen as a ritual, a way of expressing faith. Just as Christians might say a grace before meals so too did Jews at the time of Jesus, and practicing Jews today, have rituals governing their meal practice. There are various prayers of thanksgiving or blessing (*berakah*) prayed. As the meal begins bread is blessed, broken and distributed with words like the following being said: 'Blessed are you, Lord our God, eternal king, for bringing forth bread from the earth.' On feasts there would also be a blessing over wine in words such as: 'Blessed are you, Lord our God, eternal King, for making the fruit of the vine.' At the end of a meal on a solemn occasion there was a long prayer of thanksgiving, often recited over a special cup of wine which was then passed around the table (1 Cor 10:16). We can see here the roots of our practice today.

There are some things we cannot be sure of regarding this meal. Firstly scholars cannot be sure that this meal was an actual Passover meal (the gospels of Matthew, Mark and Luke think it was, but for John the meal took place on the day before the Passover, see Jn 18:28), nor can scholars be sure of who precisely was there. These factors are of interest, and indeed sometimes that which we do not know can be as important as that which we know. What is perhaps more important than seeking precision in facts is trying to understand the rich symbolic meaning attached to what happened. The Jewish people sacrifice a lamb to commemorate their liberation from slavery in Egypt (Ex 1-15; esp. 12-15), in this way reminding themselves yearly of the fact that God 'passed over' (in Hebrew *pesach*) the houses of the Jews when He slew the firstborn of Egypt, and then brought about their liberation. God is their liberator, God is faithful, and this is a constant theme in the story of the People of God. Jesus carries this covenant forward to a new degree – he becomes, for those who follow him, the paschal lamb, 'For our paschal lamb, Christ has been sacrificed' (1 Cor 5:7). It is clear that from the earliest days the meal was associated with the Passover time. This is very important when it comes to trying to understand how early Jewish-Christians understood what it was that they were doing. By keeping the connection to the *Pasch*, the Jewish Passover meal, (*Pesach seder*), Jesus can be seen as the new Paschal lamb, making a new covenant (agreement) between God and humanity. His death reconciles us to God, and his resurrection from the dead reminds us of our promise of everlasting life. This is why early Jewish-Christians gathered regularly, to remind themselves of this fact, to keep alive the memory of Jesus Christ in the celebration of the gift of his body and blood.

Early Church Practice
The fact that the followers of Jesus did this so regularly teaches us that they did not see this meal as the annual Passover one but as a new ritual, and a meal to be set in the context of the numerous meals shared between Jesus and his followers both before and after the resurrection. It was a remembrance of these fellowship meals, and at the same time a memorial of the Last Supper. This brings further challenges, for if Jesus ate with everyone, not just those who shared the customs of the Jewish people, not just those who were part of the community, what are the implications for current Eucharistic practice? Jesus practiced something we might call open table fellowship, or a 'divine indiscriminate welcome', and so we might again wonder who was at that

last meal?[2] Yes, the twelve, but the presence of other disciples, cannot be ruled out.

The earliest accounts that we have of the meetings of the followers of Jesus show us clearly that there was never an ideal celebration of the Lord's Supper. In 1 Cor 11:17-32, we see Paul incensed at what the Church in Corinth is doing. The Church has always been a gathering of saints and sinners:

> Now in the following instructions I do not commend you, because when you come together it is not for the better but for the worse. For, to begin with, when you come together as a church, I hear that there are divisions among you; and to some extent I believe it. Indeed, there have to be factions among you, for only so will it become clear who among you are genuine. When you come together, it is not really to eat the Lord's supper. For when the time comes to eat, each of you goes ahead with your own supper, and one goes hungry and another becomes drunk. What! Do you not have homes to eat and drink in? Or do you show contempt for the church of God and humiliate those who have nothing? What should I say to you? Should I commend you? In this matter I do not commend you!
>
> For I received from the Lord what I also handed on to you, that the Lord Jesus on the night when he was betrayed took a loaf of bread, and when he had given thanks, he broke it and said, 'This is my body that is for you. Do this in remembrance of me.' In the same way he took the cup also, after supper, saying, 'This cup is the new covenant in my blood. Do this, as often as you drink it, in remembrance of me.' For as often as you eat this bread and drink the cup, you proclaim the Lord's death until he comes.
>
> Whoever, therefore, eats the bread or drinks the cup of the Lord in an unworthy manner will be answerable for the body and blood of the Lord. Examine yourselves, and only then eat of the bread and drink of the cup. For all who eat and drink without discerning the body, eat and drink judgement against themselves. For this reason many of you are weak and ill, and some have died. But if

we judged ourselves, we would not be judged. But when we are judged by the Lord, we are disciplined so that we may not be condemned along with the world.

We can learn a lot from this letter of Paul to the Church at Corinth. Firstly we learn that an actual meal was shared, and an important part of the meal was the blessing of the bread and the wine, in remembrance of what the Lord Jesus had done. This meal, however, seems to have been far removed from the practice that Paul expected of followers of Christ. We read of gluttony, and of people in need being ignored. Paul admonishes the Church – this is not what the Lord meant when he said, 'Do this in remembrance of me.'

We are also reminded of the eternal dimension of the meal – in our gathering and eating we are not concerned merely with the present time but with life after death, when we will be judged, and disciplined by the Lord. We will be judged both by how we celebrate and how we live. This is the earliest description of the Lord's Supper. We can see that although the memory of Jesus' life, death and resurrection was still fresh in people's minds, it was never easy to live as a Christian.

From Meal to Formal Gathering
Sometime during the first one hundred years of Christianity, while the practice of having a meal continued, it became clearly separated from the bread and the wine ritual. The liturgy, as it developed, seemed to have allowed for a good deal of flexibility. While the core remained constant – readings, a sermon, prayers, then blessing and distribution of bread and wine – it appears that there were a great deal of regional variations in the celebrations. The question of who would preside, lead the gathering, seems to have been fluid and is a matter of some debate. People gathered in houses, and some scholarship suggests that it was the owner of the house who led the commemorative rite.

Gradually the freedom, spontaneity and fluidity disappear, and the organisational structures of surrounding cultures were adopted. Justyn Martyr (c. AD 100-165) provides an interesting account of the Eucharistic gathering in Rome around the year AD 150. We can recognise a familiar shape to the celebration:

On Sunday we have a common assembly of all our members, whether they live in the city or the outlying districts. The recollections of the apostles or the writings of the prophets are read, as long as there is time. When the reader has finished, the president of the assembly speaks to us; he urges everyone to imitate the examples of virtue we have heard in the readings. Then we all stand up together and pray.

On the conclusion of our prayer, bread and wine and water are brought forward. The president offers prayers and gives thanks to the best of his ability, and the people give assent by saying, 'Amen'. The Eucharist is distributed, everyone present communicates, and the deacons take it to those who are absent.

The wealthy, if they wish, may make a contribution, and they themselves decide the amount. The collection is placed in the custody of the president, who uses it to help the orphans and widows and all who for any reason are in distress, whether because they are sick, in prison, or away from home. In a word, he takes care of all who are in need.

A clear theological reason for their practice is articulated:

We hold our common assembly on Sunday because it is the first day of the week, the day on which God put darkness and chaos to flight and created the world, and because on that same day our saviour Jesus Christ rose from the dead. For he was crucified on Friday and on Sunday he appeared to his apostles and disciples and taught them the things that we have passed on for your consideration (*First Apology of St Justyn Martyr*, chapter 67)

By the third century amongst the Greek speaking Christians a person called the *episcopos*, overseer (secular term for anyone who had charge of a group of people), became the person who did the teaching and organising, and was also the celebrant of the liturgy, while in the Jewish-Christian community the people who did this work were termed elders, *presybteroi*. While these offices, and others, can be found in the very early Church, in for example the letters to Timothy, there is much development at this stage.[3] Over time the two structures merged, the *episcopos* became the normal presider, while the *presbyteroi* became helpers of the overseer, presiding at liturgy only in his absence. It is also interesting to note that 'for the first two centuries of Christianity, the followers of Jesus used the title "priest" only metaphorically for either Jesus as the risen Lord or for the people as a whole.'[4] The term 'priest' increasingly began to be used from the third century on for the presider at the Eucharist, but with great care as Christians wanted to ensure no confusion – no literal animal sacrifice took place in their gatherings. Jesus is the only priest, the high priest who actually sacrificed his very self thus putting an end to all further need for blood sacrifice for Christians (see the Letter to the Hebrews). Henceforth the whole people were to be a priestly people.

From Sect to Legal Religion
In the first three hundred years of Christianity it was against the law of the Empire to be a Christian, and so it remained a religion with a relatively small number of followers. This 'sect' of Judaism, was regarded as a heretical movement. This changed during the reign of Constantine (AD 306-337) when Christianity became a religion to be tolerated. For the first time it became legal to be Christian. The final significant development came when the emperor Theodosius (AD 379-395) decreed Christianity to be the legal religion of the Roman Empire. Change quickly followed. With this move, Christians quickly adapted the administration structures of the empire and the *episcopoi* became rulers and leaders in their dioceses.

We are now far from the gatherings in houses of the very early days – practically the numbers were too big. This was the era of the great basilicas, a time when a bishop (*episcopos*) was treated like an emperor. The bishop wore special clothes, marks of imperial dignity, and these became regarded as normal liturgical attire. Bishops, the leaders of Christians, were treated in this way as a mark of respect for God. While the liturgy of the Mass showed little change, celebrations became more stylised and formal. A procession, an entrance song and the *Sanctus* (song of praise), were added on by about the eight century. In the larger centres the liturgy over which the bishop presided became very much a liturgy of pomp and glory. In the country-side change occurred slowly and celebrations remained much less elaborate. While still largely married with children, the ordained were becoming increasingly separated from the rest of the church community.

The first few centuries saw many changes in practice, from a gathering of Jewish-Christians in a house for a meal to a great ceremony in a basilica, with fine vestments and clear division of roles, a division which was essentially a ranking. Slowly the service became longer. Priests now presided regularly at the Eucharist. The role of the *episcopos* changed – he became more of an administrator, increasingly removed from his people. In some places, everyone, priest included, faced eastwards as they prayed, awaiting the second coming of the Lord.

The gap between the Churches of the East (Orthodox and Oriental) and those of the West was increasing slowly, a final break would come in 1054. Latin was progressively becoming the liturgical language of the Roman Church (West) but there were still many differences in the way the Eucharist was cele-brated – we can speak of a Roman Rite, an Hispanic Rite and an Ambrosian Rite to name but a few. Unity did not mean unifor-mity. Similarly the Orthodox and Orientals had a variety of Rites – such as the Byzantine Rite, the Syrian Rite and the Armenian Rite. What was happening though, which is of partic-ular theological interest, is that the people were beginning to share communion less. While many reasons have been suggest-ed to explain this, it seems that in most cases people abstained due to a sense of personal unworthiness. The theological reasons for this are profound – the ranking in the liturgical cele-bration seems to have transferred into a ranking of holiness in people's minds. They increasingly came to recognise their unworthiness to receive something of such great holiness and wonder.[5]

Around the ninth century, a new action began to take place during the liturgy, the priest elevates the bread during the insti-tution narrative. In the tenth century the practice of elevating the chalice also begins. This was to help people to feast their eyes on the Body and Blood of Christ as few were now receiving.

'Ocular' communion was replacing eating and drinking. Priests increasingly begin to celebrate 'private masses'. The understanding of the sacrament was changing significantly.

The next major point of significance was the Council of Trent (1545-1563). Called in response to the Reformation, and seeking to address the problems highlighted by the Reformation, it gave clear instructions on many matters, and began a process which worked towards making much of the unity of the celebration of the Eucharist into uniformity. In a sense it had to do this as it sought more clarity in Church practice in an attempt to address the questions of the Reformers. Trent reaffirmed the fact that Catholics perceive the Mass as a sacrifice, and also reiterated the belief in the change of the substance of the bread and wine into the Body and Blood of Christ – 'a change most aptly termed transubstantiation'. A downside of this is that much of the diversity of rites, or differences in the liturgy, disappeared.[6] Following the Council of Trent, Pope Pius V, concerned with some innovation and accretions (additions) in the Order of the Mass, ordered a review of the Roman Missal. This revised Roman Missal was used until the Second Vatican Council. The last revision took place in 1962, and it is this revised Missal that those who celebrate the Tridentine Rite follow. The main changes of the Second Vatican Council, noticeable to the person in the pew, were the increased permission to use more of the vernacular and the fact that priests now began to celebrate Mass facing the people. Following this permission to make greater use of the vernacular, Missals in the various world languages were produced, and it became the norm to celebrate in the language of the people.

With the passage of two thousand years what is remarkable is how stable the Mass, the Eucharistic liturgy has remained. What we do today is what we read the early Christians did (Acts 2:42-47), and what Justyn Martyr described so well earlier in this chapter. Today our Eucharist is very similar, and our understanding of the Mass can be seen to have deepened over the years. With the passage of time, guided by the Holy Spirit, we grow in understanding of the richness of our sacramental tradition. Like the early followers of Jesus, we continue to gather, to give thanks, and to share in the bread and wine that will lead us to the eternal banquet. We do what they did, and we do some things they did not do. In the next two chapters we will look more closely at the Mass, the celebration of the Eucharist, and see why it is that we do what we do in the way that we do it.

CHAPTER THREE

The Table of the Word

'Ignorance of Scripture is ignorance of Christ'
St Jerome's *Commentary on Isaiah*

The Mass is central to being a Catholic, and as we have seen that which is central to the Mass has not changed significantly in two thousand years. But what is the Mass besides a gathering of people, led by a priest, who mumble some prayers and sit and kneel and stand at strange times? Were aliens to land on earth and observe a Catholic Mass I wonder what they might think? Or indeed what do people not brought up in a religious ritual tradition think about the Mass, about prayer, about liturgy? The Mass only makes sense if understood in its correct context, and this context is the people who try to continually retell the story of Jesus' life, death and resurrection so that it will never be forgotten, a story which is slowly changing them into a holy people, a people worthy of the title 'Christian', follower of Christ. Many people, especially children and young adults, claim that they find the Mass boring. Perhaps this is because their experience is too often that of a poorly celebrated ritual? Maybe they do not understand, as they have never really been taught, the rich significance of celebrating the Eucharist? The words and actions may be familiar, but perhaps not the meaning.

The Mass
The Mass can only make sense to a believer because it is always about thanksgiving, about giving thanks to God. The term Mass (*missa*) became the popular word for the celebration in the Catholic Church in the seventh century, after the time of Pope Gregory the Great (d. 604). In the early days of Christianity many terms were used such as the 'breaking of bread' (*fractio panis*), 'The Lord's Supper' (*coena dominica*), the 'Sacrifice' (*prosphora, oblatio*), 'the gathering together' (*synaxis, congregatio*), 'the Mysteries', and 'the Sacrament of the Altar'. A variety of

names were used to speak of the same thing. Similarly, today many terms are in use among Christian Churches such as the Lord's Supper, Holy Communion, and Holy Mass. The word *missa* comes from the Latin word *missio*, simply meaning a 'dismissal' (*dimissio*). This phrase, *missa est*, was originally used to release people from attendance at the emperor's courts, reminding us of how we adapted some facets of 'imperial' practice when it became legal to be a Christian (with the emperors Constantine and Theodosius in the fourth century). With the Mass this phrase brings the formal prayer to a close – *Ite missa est*, 'Go forth, the Mass is ended'. Indeed all our concluding rites command us to 'go', we are now to make incarnate in our lives that which we have just celebrated, we are to live as Christians.

Today we often refer to the Mass as the eucharistic celebration, and this book is called the Eucharist to remind us that the Mass is about much more than receiving Holy Communion. The word Eucharist comes from the Greek word *eucharistia* meaning thanksgiving, and so we gather to give thanks to God. No matter what our personal situation at that moment, we come together to give thanks. Even at a funeral of a young child, even if I have just been diagnosed with a terminal disease, I gather with other Catholics to give thanks to God for all that God has done for us. I personally may be finding it difficult to give thanks today, even to believe, but I am with fellow baptised people, and I share in their hope that there is a resurrection from the dead – Christ is risen, we too shall rise. Although individuals we are part of the Body of Christ, part of a 'we' much bigger than can ever be imagined.

The Paschal Mystery

We gather in the name of Christ to give thanks for what God has done for us in Christ, especially for his resurrection from the dead. Each time we celebrate the Eucharist we are plunged into the Paschal Mystery, into the death and glorification of Jesus Christ.[1] As St Thomas Aquinas (c.1225-1274), in his famous *Summa Theologiae*, writes, 'in this sacrament is included the whole mystery of our salvation' (*ST* III q. 83 a.4.c.). And what is 'the mystery of our salvation'? St Paul summarises it clearly in his letter to the Corinthians: 'Christ died for our sins in accordance with the scriptures, and that he was buried, and that he was raised on the third day in accordance with the scriptures' (1 Cor 15:3-4). It is the Christian hope that just as 'Christ is risen' we too shall share in this resurrection from the dead into eternal life with God once our life on earth is ended. This is the mystery of salvation remembered each time we gather to pray the Mass – for Christians, death is not the end.

Why We Do What We Do
Some key ideas underpin each Eucharist celebrated, and make it what it is. Most of these core elements have their roots in Judaic practices. Key among these is the idea of memory, memorial, *zikkaron*. A rich concept of memory is central to the Jewish people. During the Passover, *seder*, they pray that 'each of us must this night remember that he/she has come out of the land of Egypt'. In this way, through their rites and prayers, the Jewish people keep the memory of what God has done for them in the past to the forefront, and they continuously urge God to 'remember' the People of God. It is the memory of God's wonderful acts in the past (the *mirabilia Dei*), which keep alive the hope that God will again act wonderfully today, and every 'today' that the Jewish people live. God is always faithful.

This is similar to what happens when we gather to pray the Eucharist. We remember what God did in the past, in particular the fact that 'on the third day God raised Jesus Christ from the dead', and as we remember we 'remind' God and ask God to do wonderful things in our world, in our today. Because God has done as God said in the past, we trust God will act again. Like the Jewish people, our prayer is a trusting supplication in the unfailing power of the Word. God's Word created the world (Gen 1, 'God said') and lived among us ('and the Word became flesh', Jn 1:14).[2] In our eucharistic gatherings, we 'remind' God of the fidelity of His promise to save us. We 'remind' God, and ourselves, that 'Christ has died, Christ is risen, Christ will come again'. We pray in a sense 'so that he will come'. We pray so that we may truly become the Body and Blood of Christ. In our baptism we were baptised into the Body of Christ, through our eucharistic celebrations we grow into the fulfilment of that mysterious membership.

The Greek term for memorial is *anamnesis,* and this word is often used by liturgical theologians when they try to explain what the Mass is about. *Anamnesis* is really for Christians what *zikkaron* is for Jews – a liturgical memorial which renders present the past actions of God as a living reality for the worshipper. During the Christian Eucharist we make present something from the past; we remember the story of Jesus 'as if' it was happening now, in our time. We pray the Mass remembering that the life, death, resurrection and ascension are one complex act, which occurred in history, but with effect 'now'.

> The Eucharistic memorial is celebrated in fidelity to Jesus' command. It is no mere calling to mind of a past event. It is the Church's effectual proclamation of God's reconciling action in Christ. Through it, we not only recall Jesus Christ's Passion on behalf of the whole Church but we participate 'today' in these benefits and enter into the movement of his self-offering. Through the power of the Spirit, the once and for all event of Jesus' Death on the Cross is made present in our time in each Mass. We become present to that great event and are bound together in communion by it, not only with those we meet in any particular Mass, but with those gathered around the Eucharist in all corners of the world and throughout time.[3]

In the Name of the Trinity

On entering the Church, Catholics bless themselves with Holy Water. This practice is a very profound one, although we can often do it without thinking. It is a regular reminder of our entry into the Catholic Church, a memory of our baptism when we were initiated into the People of God by a blessing with Holy Water and in the name of the Trinity. It is a wonderful act, beautifully encapsulated in the words of Charles Péguy:

> As at the entrance of the church on Sunday and on the feast days,
> When we go to Mass,
> Or at funerals,
> We give each other, we pass each other the holy water from hand to hand.

From neighbour to neighbour, one after the other.
Directly from hand to hand or from a blessed branch
dipped into the holy water.
In order to make the sign of the cross either over our-
selves, who are alive, or over the casket of the person who
has died,
In such a way that the same sign of the cross is as if car-
ried from neighbour to neighbour by the same water,
By the ministry, by the administering of the same water,
One after the other, over the same breasts and over the
same hearts,
And the same foreheads too,
And even over the caskets of the same deceased bodies,
So from hand to hand, from finger to finger
From fingertip to fingertip, the eternal generations,
Who are eternally going to Mass,
In the same breasts, in the same hearts up to the death of
the world, like a relay,
In the same hope, the word of God is passed on.[4]

We begin each Eucharistic celebration by again signing ourselves with the sign of the cross, thus reminding ourselves that
though we call ourselves Christians, the God we worship is the
God Jesus Christ 'introduced' us to, the God that is Trinitarian,
three in one, the God revealed in the story of Jesus' baptism by
John: 'And when Jesus had been baptised, just as he came up
from the water, suddenly the heavens were opened to him and
he saw the Spirit of God descending like a dove and alighting on
him. And a voice from heaven said, "This is my Son, the
Beloved, with whom I am well pleased"' (Matt 3:16-17). The
God we give thanks to is Father, Son and Holy Spirit, the God
we call upon is Father, Son and Holy Spirit.

Forgiven Sinner
We gather to give thanks for the fact that we are forgiven sinners, sinners most definitely but forgiven because of Jesus'
death on the cross. The celebration of the Mass reminds us of
this, and indeed the celebration of the Mass itself forgives sin. In
a sense we could say that we are made worthy to receive Holy

Communion during the Mass for 'this sacrament has from Christ's passion the power of forgiving all sins' (Thomas Aquinas, *Summa Theologiae* III q.79, a.3).[5] This is a tremendous statement. It reminds us of God's abounding love for each one of us, and of the greatness of the Eucharistic celebration. We gather together in love because God has invited us, and God makes us worthy. We could never do it ourselves, we cannot earn forgiveness or salvation, we can only accept is as a gift, what we traditionally called grace. Our role is to do the best we can to prepare ourselves to be able to receive the gift, to be open to God's presence in our lives and this calls us to pray and to learn about God through reading sacred scripture, Church teaching like the documents of Vatican II and good books on our faith, theology books. As we come to know God more we will grow in love of God and increased awe and wonder at the great gift the Eucharist is to us.

The whole of our celebration of the Eucharist is a reminder of the fact that we are forgiven sinners. Mass normally begins with the Penitential Act, where we confess our sins and ask for God's mercy. Sometimes on Sundays, in place of the Penitential Act, we may have a blessing and sprinkling with water to remind us of our baptism, of our being plunged for the first time into the Paschal Mystery, into the mystery of our salvation. During the Penitential Act one person, the priest, prays the words of absolution, asking for God's mercy and forgiveness, and for the gift of eternal life for all of us. On Sundays when we pray the creed we confess this belief in the forgiveness of sins, and then when we come to the Our Father this plea for the forgiveness of sin is repeated. The Our Father reminds the community that communion, peace with God, implies peace with one another – forgive us as we forgive others. Forgiveness of sin is like a refrain running through all celebrations of the Eucharist.

But where does this put confession, the sacrament of reconciliation? This very wonderful gift to the Church is an important sacrament in its own right, not merely as an entry point to Holy Communion, and more needs to be done to develop the richness of this sacrament. The sacrament of reconciliation provides another great opportunity to celebrate God's forgiveness, it also gives Catholics a chance to speak with the security of full confidentiality about things which may be worrying us, aspects of our living with which we are not happy. For those of us who may be aware that we have committed 'mortal sin', that is sin that cuts us off from God, Church teaching obliges us to celebrate the sacrament of reconciliation as an essential part of the process of bringing us back to full communion with God and with one another.[6] As the *Catechism of the Catholic Church* teaches: 'Anyone conscious of a grave sin must receive the sacrament of Reconciliation before coming to communion' (n. 1385).

Forgiveness of sin is another way of saying that God is faithful, God is with us no matter what we do, and thus the next thing we do is to sing or say the *Gloria*, that great hymn of praise to God. In this prayer we thank God for the forgiveness of sin, for the gift of redemption. Next the priest invites the gathered community to a brief silence so that we can become more intensely aware of being in God's presence. Then he pronounces the prayer called the *Collect* which, by ancient tradition, is usually addressed to God the Father, through Christ, in the Holy Spirit. At the end we all acclaim Amen assenting that this is the God we believe in.

All that we have spoken of thus far is a preparation for the main part of the celebration. The preparatory period of recognition of sinfulness and the rendering of glory to God leads firstly into the Liturgy of the Word, and then the Liturgy of the Eucharist. *The General Instruction on the Roman Missal* (GIRM) tells us that these two parts of the Eucharistic celebration are 'so closely interconnected that they form but one single act of worship' (GIRM 28).[7]

Liturgy of the Word
What Christians do here is not unlike what Jews do in their synagogue services today, and what Jesus and his followers would have done in their time. We listen to Scriptures being proclaimed. The difference is that Christians have many more books to their Scriptures than the Jewish people have. Fundamentally though, the practice is the same – we all listen to the story of God and God's relationship with the People of God. The story we hear proclaimed is one of enduring faithfulness, and of a God of love. The fundamental truth of our human

existence is that each one of us has been created after the image and likeness of God (Gen 1:26-27) and the whole of our religious life and practice is an attempt to grow more and more into that image and likeness. The story of the Bible is the story of a people's response to this invitation of God to become holy – 'as he who called you is holy, be holy yourselves in all your conduct; for it is written, "You shall be holy, for I am holy"' (1 Pet 1:15-16).[8] This call is found in both the Jewish Scriptures and the Christian Scriptures.

The Bible, from which the Scripture readings are chosen, is the inspired Word of God, and for Christians consists of what we call the Old and the New Testament (many Scripture scholars today prefer to call them the First Testament and the Second Testament). It consists of a closed number of writings deemed to have been composed under divine inspiration and destined to help the Church to grow in holiness.[9] The message of the Bible is simple yet deep – God is the Creator of all that is, and God created humankind for the sake of eternal life with God. For Christians, this message is proclaimed most clearly in the life of Jesus Christ.

In the Catholic Sunday Eucharist the first reading is normally from the Old Testament, the story of God and the Jewish people, except during Eastertide when it is taken from the Acts of the Apostles, the story of the beginning of the Church. The Second Reading is always from the New Testament. In between both readings we pray a psalm. Sometimes the psalm seems to slip by unnoticed but these prayers would merit a lot more attention as they speak to every human emotion – joy, sadness, despair and happiness. When we pray the psalms we are using God's word to respond to God's word. These prayers, so central to the Jewish people are also prayed daily by many Christians, especially in religious communities when they gather to pray the Divine Office of the Church.[10] They are beautiful prayers that we should not reserve solely to the Mass. The third reading we hear is the Gospel, the Good News of Jesus' life, death and resurrection.

The Scriptures nourish our minds and our prayers, and it is important that we listen attentively. The Word of God which is proclaimed is God speaking to us, here and now, as if we were present when these words were first said. They speak to the listener of God's faithfulness and God's great love for each one of us personally revealed in Christ. For this reason the responsibility that goes with being a reader, a proclaimer of Scripture at Mass, is a very precious one. The Second Vatican Council, in its great document on the liturgy, *Sacrosanctum Concilium* (*SC*), reminded us of the great gift our scripture is when it declared that Christ 'is present in His word, since it is He Himself who speaks when the holy Scriptures are read in the Church' (*SC*, 7). It is Christ himself who speaks when the holy Scriptures are read in the Church. This is truly amazing and puts a whole new focus on our attentiveness to the Word, and also on the need for people to proclaim this Word with authority. Although a person might be able to read, not everyone has the charism of proclaiming God's Word. While the Second Vatican Council is clear that we are all called to active participation in the life of the Church, and especially in the liturgy, we are not all gifted in the same way. Formation is needed, as is courageous discernment as to who may, or may not proclaim God's Word to the gathered assembly. The priority must always be that the Word of God be clearly audible so that the gathered community can hear what God is saying to us today, 'now', in 1378, or in 1876, or in 2012, or 3089. It is the same God addressing us with a constant message, a constant call to become holier.

Breaking of the Word

To help the people gathered to understand more deeply the message of God, the proclamation of the Scriptures is followed by what has traditionally been termed the homily. Today many people like to call it the 'breaking of the Word'. Just as we will soon have the 'breaking of the Bread', in this part of the Eucharist we have the 'breaking of the Word'. Christ is present in both Word and Bread, nourishing us in our minds and in our bodies. This is an opportunity to have the Scriptures explained, to have them put in context, and made sense of, for today. The 'breaking of the Word' is a very important part of the liturgy as God's Word needs explanation. While Scripture, the Bible, is indeed the inspired Word of God, we Catholics believe that it is always in the context of the whole story, which comes to its climax in the story of Jesus, that each part is to be understood. The complexity of the story in Scripture needs much study if it is to be preached on effectively. For this reason, those delegated to preach must be willing to read and study the Scriptures, and then explain and make it relevant to our lives, today, in the twenty-first century. The preacher's task is a difficult one: to address a wide variety of people, of all ages and interests. The homily is not a class on Scripture, this can and should take place in a Bible studies class, but literally a 'breaking of the Word' into understandable and tasty morsels for all people. The taste may vary as God's message, while always one of constant loving presence, is simultaneously a call to conversion, to change, to *metanoia*.[11]

While ordinarily it is the ordained person who preaches, Canon Law permits others to 'preach in a church or oratory if in certain circumstances it is necessary, or in particular cases it would be advantageous, according to the provisions of the Episcopal Conference' (Canon 766). There is a distinction made between the homily, part of the liturgy and reserved to a priest or deacon (Canon 767), and the ability to preach, which as we have seen can be given by a lay person. Today one must wonder if this is essential. Many very good ordained ministers do not have the charism of being able to give an effective homily, and many laity are now very well formed theologically, and are also effective communicators. Perhaps we need changed norms to guide us, keeping in mind that the truth that God is love needs to be proclaimed, and that effective preaching of this must take priority. The role of preaching must be safeguarded, for it is indeed a frightening responsibility, but perhaps norms from the past need readdressing. People are hungry to hear the Word of God proclaimed and explained. I think of a friend, an academic theologian who frequently preaches in other Christian churches but has never been invited to do so in his own, the Catholic Church.

We Believe

Next we move onto the Liturgy of the Eucharist, but on Sundays and holy days before we do this we recite together the great profession of our faith, the Creed. The Creed contains the essential truths of Christian faith. Nicholas Lash, a great English theologian and author of many books, insightfully wrote, 'what the Scriptures say at length, the creed says briefly.'[12] The essentials, or essence of Christian faith, are indeed short: God is Trinity, Father, Son and Holy Spirit. The Father, the Creator, sent the Son to dwell among us; crucified and raised up from the dead, he breathed the Holy Spirit, the sanctifier, upon us. The Son, who has known our human condition, will judge us in a Godly way when our life on earth is ended. We also profess belief in the Catholic Church, the communion of saints, and again in the forgiveness of sins, and in life everlasting. These amazing truths were put together into this great prayer very early on in our story. They were developed from the practice at baptisms of asking the people being baptised to affirm their faith in the teachings of the Catholic Church, not unlike the process followed when we renew our baptismal vows. This reminding and repeating is an important part of the Catholic practice.

The eucharistic celebration is essentially a constant reminding of what God has done for 'us', the People of God in the past, so that our security, our trust in God grows. The God who raised Jesus Christ from the dead, the one we will later address as Our Father, is to be trusted. God's Word is always effective; what God says, God does. In a sense as we remember the great works of God in the past, we also seek to remind God of what has been done for us. We thank God for this, and we do this as we plead with God, pray to God, to do again these great things in our days. The next part of the liturgy is where this concretely happens, in faith we believe that just as God's Word was effective in creating the whole world, and just as God's power was able to raise someone from the dead, now too, today, here in this gathering, God will change the bread and wine into the Body and Blood of His Son. This is what we believe happens in the Liturgy of the Eucharist.

CHAPTER FOUR

When do you eat your God?

'Those who eat my flesh and drink my blood
abide in me, and I in them' (Jn 6:56)

A friend once recounted a valuable learning experience of hers. She used to give hospitality every summer to a student from overseas, young students who had come to improve their English. She enjoyed having them, learning about their cultures, and at the same time augmenting her income. Once she had an Indian student to stay; he wasn't a Christian but he went along with her to Mass. At one stage during the Mass he asked her, in total innocence, 'when do you eat your God'?

This is indeed a remarkable question, which reminds us that that which we claim to do is understandably strange to the outsider. Indeed what do we do, or claim to do? Our minds having been nourished, we proceed as a community to what is termed the Liturgy of the Eucharist. What happens here is quite simple, and at once most profound, and as we have seen, it makes no sense to someone outside the story. It is indeed 'non-sense'. We have heard the story of God's faithfulness to people throughout history, firstly to the Jewish people through their many struggles, and then of God's faithfulness to the followers of Jesus – God raised Jesus from the dead. No matter what we do, have done, or indeed fail to do, the message is clear. Even when we crucified the Son of God on a cross, the truth remains that God is with us and will respond to our cry if we can but trust. Psalm 78 is one of the many places in Scripture where we are reminded of God's constancy:

> Their heart was not steadfast towards God;
> they were not true to God's covenant.
> Yet God, being compassionate,
> forgave their iniquity,
> and did not destroy them;

often God restrained his anger,
and did not stir up all his wrath.
God remembered that they were but flesh,
a wind that passes and does not come again.
(Ps 78:37-39)

As we have seen in chapter three, *anamnesis* (memorial) is central to what we do at Eucharist. As we remind ourselves of the stories of God's faithfulness in the proclaiming of Sacred Scripture we are also, one might say, in a sense, 'reminding' God of God's faithfulness. We are saying 'God, you did these great things for our ancestors in the past, do them again in our time, now, in our Eucharistic celebration, answer our plea'. We know we can trust God because we have experienced God's fidelity in the stories we recall. And our plea, our prayer is straightforward – send your Holy Spirit and change this bread and this wine into the Body and Blood of your Son Jesus Christ, the long awaited Messiah, so that we can all receive Christ in Holy Communion.[1] Send your Holy Spirit on us so that we, your people, might become more truly the Body of Christ. Simple, yet most profound, it is indeed an everyday miracle.

We Pray, We Beseech, We Remember

This phase of the Eucharist begins with the procession of the gifts of bread and wine to the altar. We return to God what God has gifted to us, but we return them to God after we have made them our own. God created them, as God has created all that is, and we have been invited into God's work, we have become co-creators, or perhaps better put 'makers'. From grain and grape we have made bread and wine, and now we pray that they will become for us, spiritual food and spiritual drink. We have our beautiful Eucharistic Prayers, a rich inheritance with roots in the Jewish tradition, and in the early Christian Church. While things have changed a little with the passage of time, and so we cannot truthfully identify the 'original' words, and aware that we are always working with translated texts, what we do has largely remained the same since earliest times. It is 'we' who do it.[2] At times it can seem that, because from now on the presider (priest) does most of the talking, we might as well not be there, our role is not important. This is not the case. We are part of the Body of Christ and our absence leaves the Body bereft, in some way deficient. Full active participation, the expressed desire of the Second Vatican Council does not mean that everyone does everything. During the Eucharistic prayer while one person vocalises most of the words, he speaks on our behalf. The prayers are in the plural – 'we make humble prayer and petition', 'we celebrate the memorial of the blessed Passion', 'Make holy, therefore, these gifts, we pray', 'Have mercy on us all, we pray', 'May he make of us an eternal offering to you', 'We give you praise, Father most holy, for you are great'. It is the People of God, the baptised, who have gathered to give thanks to God, who now beseech the Holy One to accept our offering of bread and wine and to send the Holy Spirit to sanctify, to make holy these gifts, so that they 'may become the body and blood of our Lord Jesus Christ'. We ask for no small thing, we ask for a miracle, and we ask confident that the 'miracle' will occur, for God is faithful.

This we do, this we can do, because of the Last Meal that Jesus shared with his followers, his disciples. When we gather for our Eucharist we must remember that we gather in the tradition of all the meals that Jesus shared with his followers (see chapter five), and the meals shared with those who were not yet his followers. The last meal, however is of pre-eminent importance, and we recall this meal particularly. When we move onto the prayer which recalls the event of this last meal, we use words based on those found in scripture (Mt 26:26-29; Mk 14:22-25; Lk 22:14-23; 1 Cor 11:23-26). We move to the language of the past as we recount an event that is past, an historic event that is of everlasting consequence. Jesus took, blessed, broke, and gave. In remembering what happened, we are also proclaiming what is happening and will happen till the end of time. We can do this because we are confident of God's faithfulness, and God's presence, and God's gift of God's very self to us. This is indeed an amazing thing.

It is important to remember that while the story is the celebration of the last meal that Jesus celebrated with his followers, it is so much more. Together with the story of the death on a cross and the resurrection from the dead it is the story of salvation, the promise of salvation for all. In a sense it is the pivot around which all of history turns for Christians. The Eucharist is a celebration of a belief in a life after death, and no less a celebration of the goodness of matter. It is good to be human, and it is good to be bread, or wine. All of matter is good, for all has been created by God. In the book of Genesis, God judges all that has been created as good, and very good (Gen 1).

An Act of God

At the beginning of the Eucharistic Prayer we offer bread and wine to God, and at the end we receive the body and blood of Christ. A profound change has taken place: matter, which is good, has been 'changed' into the Body and Blood of Christ, it has been divinised. Catholics use the term 'transubstantiation' to try to explain this mysterious change (we will discuss this in more detail in chapter seven). We need to be careful here and to remember that we are not defining what happens, this is not an occurrence at the level of scientific change, but an act of God in history. Human words can never adequately explain it. What we do know, and accept in faith, is that while the bread still looks like bread, and the wine like wine, they have now become for us the body and blood of Christ (Eucharistic Prayer II). While we are rightly amazed at this great act, this 'everyday miracle', St Ambrose of Milan (c.339-397), seeking to explain to his people what happens, reminds us that while we are right to wonder, this is what our God does. It is our minds that are limited. 'Surely,' he wrote, 'the word of Christ, which could make out of nothing that which did not exist, can change things already in existence into what they were not.' Indeed, nothing is impossible to God. Bread and wine become, in a way we cannot understand, 'the Body and Blood of Christ' (*On the Mysteries*, chapter 4, n.52).

Amen

Each of our Eucharistic prayers comes to completion with the wonderful doxology of praise to our God who is Trinity, and the final word, a word of only four letters but perhaps the most powerful word of all our prayers, *Amen*. This little word says almost everything we need to say. 'It is a people-binding act, a pledge of solidarity with the purposes and promises of God.'[3] It comes at key points in our liturgy, and occurs so often that it can often be thoughtlessly said, and so not be the act of faith it might be. Our *Amen*, whenever we say it, is always an acknowledgment of God's *Amen*, God's Yes, which always precedes our Yes. It is because of God's Yes that we stutter our 'yes', our *Amen*, our response of commitment to God. This is our constant tradition and is marvellously articulated in Paul's letter to the Corinthians:

> As surely as God is faithful, our word to you has not been 'Yes and No.' For the Son of God, Jesus Christ, whom we proclaimed among you, Silvanus and Timothy and I, was not 'Yes and No'; but in him it is always 'Yes.' For in him every one of God's promises is a 'Yes.' For this reason it is through him that we say the 'Amen,' to the glory of God. But it is God who establishes us with you in Christ and has anointed us, by putting his seal on us and giving us his Spirit in our hearts as a first instalment (2 Cor 1:18-22).

God's promise is a 'Yes' and so we can say *Amen*.

Before we say *Amen* and receive Holy Communion we remind ourselves once more of God's great love, which always enfolds our sinfulness as we recite together the 'Our Father'. This, 'most perfect' of prayers says everything that needs to be said, encapsulating all that has been said.[4] Speaking about the 'Our Father', St Teresa of Avila advises:

> The sublimity of the perfection of this evangelical prayer is something for which we should give great praise to the Lord … I am astounded when I consider that in its few words are enshrined all contemplation and perfection, so that if we study it no other book seems necessary.[5]

Our prayers, while we use many words, are simply reiterating over and over again the same message: God is Love, and though we often fall short, love and forgiveness is God's constant response. We are called, in so far as we are able, to be agents of God's love and forgiveness in the world. During the Mass, a great opportunity to be an active agent of this love comes at the time of the sign of peace and so as we offer one another the sign of peace we should seek to do this in a 'godly' fashion. This is an opportunity to begin once more to live out our Eucharistic life. Christ is present in each person gathered here for this liturgy today – so as we offer our neighbour the sign of peace let us do so with reverence, recognising, or at least trying to recognise, the presence of Christ in the other person, as they mutually acknowledge Christ's presence in me. This is no simple handshake (or whatever the appropriate gesture is in the culture), this is a profound expression of faith in the God who created humankind after God's image and likeness. I am the Body of Christ, and so are you. This is what we seek to proclaim.

Invited to His Supper
As a member of the Body of Christ we are next invited to receive, we are 'called to his supper'. The response to this invitation, 'Lord I am not worthy' is the truth. No one is. Yet, as St Alphonsus Liguori (1696-1787) pondered:

> But what are the proper dispositions? If they understand by this that we should be worthy, who would ever be allowed to approach Holy Communion? Only Jesus Christ could worthily receive the Eucharist since only God could worthily receive God (*Directions of Souls Who Wish to Lead a Deeply Spiritual Life*, paragraph 30).

None of us are worthy, and yet we are all invited. It is by receiving that we slowly become changed, slowly we become worthier in so far as we allow ourselves to be opened to God's transforming presence in our lives.

Receiving is not magic. God's grace never forces itself. So while the Church correctly teaches that sacraments 'are efficacious because in them Christ himself is at work' (*Catechism of the Catholic Church*, n. 1127), it also stresses the fact that in order for sacraments to confer the grace which they signify they must be celebrated worthily, in faith. While the language is less welcoming the Council of Trent is also clear about this – sacraments contain the grace which they signify and thus confer grace on those who do not place an obstacle to God, to grace.[6]

Unworthy though we are, we are welcome. We know this because of the story of God's fidelity to the People of God throughout the Old Testament, and because of Jesus' practice of associating with everyone. The gospels continually remind the Christian of Jesus' practice of table fellowship. To be a follower of Jesus does not seem to have been perceived as demanding high standards of living, at least initially: 'Now all the tax-collectors and sinners were coming near to listen to him. And the Pharisees and the scribes were grumbling and saying, "This fellow welcomes sinners and eats with them"' (Lk 15: 1-2).

Although we are unworthy we are called to become worthy, to become holy, to grow more and more into God's image and likeness. This we begin again each time we celebrate the Eucharist, as we try to pray each eucharistic celebration 'better', for want of a more suitable word.[7] We give physical witness to this in our bodies and our stance during the liturgy – whether standing, sitting or kneeling. While there are Instructions on stance during the liturgy there is an argument to be made against the practice of kneeling during the Eucharist. Kneeling is a penitential act, and while we are sinners we come to celebrate the fact that we are forgiven sinners, that we are even now, living the beginnings of our resurrected life. Kneeling is also more suitable for private prayer, and the Eucharist is a public prayer of the Church. On the other hand, standing is the stance of a resurrected and saved people; it is the way Jewish people pray when they gather in their synagogues, and so was the way Jesus and his followers would have prayed. The priest stands leading us in prayer, were we to stand with him we would better express the unity of the Body of Christ, the People of God.

Another instance where our physical stance is of great importance is when we come forward to receive. We should ensure that we come forward with reverence, in a gentle manner. There is no need to rush, there will be plenty. Each community has the responsibility to organise the procession forward to receive in a manner which permits people to come forward with dignity. While the whole liturgy is one, this is a unique moment where we individually proclaim our faith. What we are about to do marks a very special moment and so when we receive Christ in the consecrated species we should do so with great dignity. Whether we receive in our hands or on our tongue, dignity and respect must be maintained. Indeed as adults meeting their God, it might be deemed more appropriate to 'receive' bread into one's hands, for only babies are fed into their mouth, and indeed in the early Church to receive in one's hands was the practice. The practice of receiving Holy Communion on the tongue reflects a later development in faith and theology which stressed people's unworthiness to receive, their unworthiness to touch the consecrated Host. It came to be understood that laity would show greater respect and more humility by receiving on the tongue, only the priest was sufficiently holy to touch the consecrated elements.[8]

More recent theology reminds us that all of us gathered are consecrated to the God who is Trinity by our baptism. The role of the priest is indeed specific but not necessarily holier. Perhaps our understanding of priesthood needs some more consideration. This, however, is beyond the scope of this present book. For now we must agree that there is an option, and however we receive, let us do so with dignity. The words of the fourth-century bishop, St Cyril of Alexandria (c.376-444), speak primarily of reverence, of respect:

> Make your left hand a throne for your right, since your right hand is about to welcome a king. Cup your palm and receive in it Christ's body, saying in response 'Amen' ... then ... go to receive the chalice of his blood. (*Catechetical Lecture*, 23).

Heavenly Banquet

This teaching informs us that in the early Church it was normal practice to receive from the cup. Again with the passage of time reception on the tongue, and the withdrawal of the chalice from the laity, became the tradition. The Second Vatican Council, following the teachings of the Council of Trent, tried to recover this practice of receiving under both kinds. The *General Instruction on the Roman Missal* teaches that while Christ, whole and entire, is received even in only one species, Holy Communion has a fuller form when it is received under both kinds. When both consecrated wine and consecrated bread are received, more powerful expression is given to the sacrificial nature of the Mass.[9] To ensure this becomes a real option for people an adequate number of chalices need to provided, ordinarily two Eucharistic Ministers of the Chalice to accompany each Eucharistic Minister of the Host. It does indeed involve more people, and more work, but ensuring that the Body of Christ is received in its fullest form should be important for each community. What we are receiving is a foretaste of the eschatological feast (from the Greek *eschata* meaning last things, death and its aftermath), the heavenly banquet we shall all share in the Kingdom of God. Each Eucharistic meal is a reminder of our hope, our sure and certain hope, that God will raise us to eternal life. This is the promise of scripture, of God.

> Those who eat my flesh and drink my blood have eternal life, and I will raise them up on the last day; for my flesh is true food and my blood is true drink. Those who eat my flesh and drink my blood abide in me, and I in them. Just as the living Father sent me, and I live because of the Father, so whoever eats me will live because of me. This is the bread that came down from heaven, not like that which your ancestors ate, and they died. But the one who eats this bread will live for ever (Jn 6:54-58).

In a sense we are eating and drinking our way to eternal life. It is a profound act we engage in. Once again that little word *Amen* is of great significance. St Augustine (354-430), in a homily given one Easter Sunday to those who had been initiated (baptised, confirmed and received Holy Communion) on Holy Saturday night, explains the wonderful mystery they have been initiated into:

> So now, if you want to understand the body of Christ, listen to the Apostle Paul speaking to the faithful: 'You are the body of Christ, member for member' (1 Cor 12:27). If you, therefore, are Christ's body and members, it is your own mystery that is placed on the Lord's table! It is your own mystery that you are receiving! You are saying 'Amen' to what you are: your response is a personal signature, affirming your faith. When you hear 'The body of Christ', you reply 'Amen.' Be a member of Christ's body, then, so that your 'Amen' may ring true! (*Sermon* 272).

A Eucharistic Ecclesiology

In this wonderful teaching we see the beginnings of a Eucharistic ecclesiology, a vision of Church rooted in a rich understanding of Eucharist. 'Be a member of Christ's body, then, so that your "Amen" may ring true.' This is the invitation, and the challenge. It is fitting to give time to allow us to ponder, to contemplate this great mystery and so a period of silence, and individual prayer, is part of the post communion time. The importance of silence can never be overestimated. Scripture continually reminds us that God likes to speak to us in silence. If we want to hear, therefore, we must allow for silence. This time also allows us to prepare ourselves to get ready to leave this gathering, this liturgical celebration, and now go forward with thanksgiving (*eucharistia*) in our hearts 'to glorify the Lord with our lives.'

CHAPTER FIVE

Eucharist – The Sacrament of Divine Indiscriminate Welcome?

'Jesus said to them, "Come and have breakfast."
… Jesus came and took the bread and gave it to
them, and did the same with the fish'
(Jn 21:12–13)

The Eucharist is indeed a great gift to the Church. As we pray our eucharistic liturgy we remember not only the great story of the Paschal Mystery, of the death and resurrection of Jesus, but we also remember the story of Jesus' life. It is the whole of his life story which is to us an example of how to live as Christians, of how to live eucharistically. We are drawn into his life story so that, by the gift of the Holy Spirit, we come to live as he did.

Central to the Gospels' account of Jesus are a series of meals, and it is noted by the writers that the invitation was wide open; tax-collectors, women, sinners of all sorts, prostitutes (Mt 9:10-13; Mk 2:15-17; Lk 5:29-32) all ate with Jesus. We read accounts of Jesus eating with his friends (Jn 12:1-2), and with leaders of the Jewish community (Lk 7:36). We also read of Jesus generously feeding others, many others, with loaves and fishes (Mk 6; Lk 9:10-17). Jesus enjoyed being with people, eating with them. It seems that when it came to accepting and sharing hospitality Jesus exercised what might be termed a 'divine indiscriminate welcome'. Even the last meal that he shared with his disciples involved him sharing bread with those who would betray him (Judas) and deny him (Peter). These stories are recounted not only to call to mind the practice of Jesus but to recall to the centre of our faith the significance of this wide open invitation: 'Jesus proclaims the indefeasible and indiscriminate and indestructible regard of God for all, regardless of merit and achievement.'[1] Jesus' invitation is wide open because God's love is wide open. His table fellowship met with opposition. Many of the parables are probably Jesus' attempt to explain, to offer a defence. Most prominent here is the story of the Prodigal Son (Lk 15:1-20) where the father is described as rushing out to meet his homecoming son, even before the son gets to say a word. It is also in the background of many of Jesus' most memorable sayings such as, 'God sends his rain on the righteous and the unrighteous' (Mt 5:45).

The question and the challenge for the early Church was how to continue to witness to the divine indiscriminate welcome as Jesus did. It was the issue at the heart of St Paul's mission to the Gentiles. This is still the question, the challenge to the People of God in every generation, and in our time too. How do we, as Church, continue to witness the divine indiscriminate welcome as Jesus did?

Inclusions and Exclusions
Many different groups spring to mind in any discussion of Eucharistic welcome, of Eucharistic inclusion and exclusion.[2] Some groups such as non-Roman Catholic Christians and Catholics in what is termed 'irregular' situations come to mind immediately. Another group, and perhaps the largest group, is less often considered, that is those who live in areas where there is no Eucharist because the requirements for ordination cannot be met. They have catechists who teach and bring the community together to pray, but cannot celebrate the Eucharist as the catechist is not ordained and probably cannot be because they are married, or maybe they are female. This large body of Christians, while they will not be considered in this chapter, present a 'problem' that needs addressing. The Eucharist defines the core of one's identity as a Catholic, if one cannot regularly access the Eucharist can one really call oneself a Catholic?

Keeping all this in the background it must be remembered that the problems posed are complex and do not admit of easy solution. This chapter will seek to inform the reader regarding Church teaching on the first two areas of exclusion identified, and simultaneously to do some theological interpretation of the teachings, bearing in mind the challenge to each one of us individually, and to the Church as the Body of Christ, to continually ask ourselves how closely do we and our practices image the

Christ we receive. How well do we 'do this in memory of me'? In short are our Eucharistic celebrations truthful to the Trinitarian God we profess to follow? We all know people in these situations, and we must all be ready to give an account for our faith and our practices, in an informed and prayerful way, and perhaps also in a critical fashion.

With Other Christians
The sharing of eucharistic table fellowship with other Christians has been much discussed since the Second Vatican Council. The step which opened the door to this discussion was the progress made by many Christian churches in recognising each others' baptism. Today all those who have been baptised with water and in the name of the Trinity are recognised as Christians by the Catholic Church. This is wonderful and a true step on the journey toward fulfilling Christ's wish that 'all may be one' (Jn 17:21). However a problem immediately follows. Ordinarily baptism is regarded as the entry point to sharing at the communion table. Baptism finds its completion in the Eucharist, or so we proclaim. In the early Church, as we have seen, baptism and anointing were immediately followed by eucharistic sharing, it was only later that we began to separate out baptism, confirmation and Eucharist. Slowly they became recognised as separate sacraments.[3] Today, when an adult wishes to become a Christian they follow a programme called the Rite of Christian Initiation of Adults, which culminates in their receiving the sacraments of initiation, baptism, confirmation and Eucharist at the Easter Vigil liturgy on Holy Saturday night. When we baptise our babies we baptise them confident that one day they will make their first Holy Communion and we shall all be able to go to Holy Communion together, to share what theologians call Eucharistic table fellowship.

This recognition of the baptism of other Christian denominations has left the Roman Catholic Church with a dilemma. We say that baptism finds its completion in the Eucharist, so if we recognise a person's baptism should we not be glad to share Eucharist with them, either to welcome them to 'Catholic' Eucharist or to be free to share 'their' Eucharist? This is a real problem, one in need of constant attention until we have arrived at a situation where we can truly express Christian unity by sharing communion.

The Second Vatican Council

To try to explore this problematic area it is necessary to look in some detail at various teachings of the Church. While at times this reading may seem a little technical, and somewhat subtle, it is necessary as the question is complex and admits of no easy solution. What is interesting to note, as we look at the various teachings, is how teachings can change, and vary somewhat, with the passage of time, even in the short time span since the Second Vatican Council. Changes may be subtle, and yet of deep significance. It is our responsibility to enlighten ourselves so that we can make informed decisions regarding the implementation and application of these teachings, in our own lives and in the lives of those who seek our advice.

The first document that needs to be considered is the Second Vatican Council's great decree on ecumenism, *Unitatis Redintegratio* (*UR*, 1964), which begins: 'The restoration of unity (*unitatis redintegratio*) among all Christians is one of the principal concerns of the Second Vatican Council. Christ the Lord founded one Church and one Church only' (*UR* 1). The current situation of division is recognised as wrong as it 'openly contradicts the will of Christ, scandalizes the world, and damages the holy cause of preaching the Gospel to every creature' (*UR* 1). It is clear that the Catholic Church is taking the ecumenical journey very seriously. This document marked a real turning point in relations with other Christians and opened the door to conversation. The contrast with the situation before the Second Vatican Council is stark. This had been a time when Catholics rarely darkened the door of a Protestant church, when Catholics in Ireland had to request special permission from the Archbishop of Dublin to study at Trinity College Dublin, and when that famous Roman Catholic boycott of Protestant businesses took place in the 1950s in Fethard-on-Sea, Wexford.[4]

The Catholic Church has, under the guidance of the Holy Spirit, come a long way since then. So, for the most part, the ecumenical (ecumenism is the word used to describe the fostering of relationships among Christians) movement is healthy. Christians talk to one another, and frequently pray together, not least for Christian unity. From the point of view of Eucharistic table fellowship, of actually sharing Holy Communion, things are a lot more complex. While Christians can and should pray together, worship in common is not, according to the teaching of the Second Vatican Council, 'to be used indiscriminately for the restoration of unity among Christians' (*UR* 8). This is an important point and to a large degree this viewpoint continues to govern current (2012) practice. It means that amidst all the positive steps, all the praying together, we are still not as one as we might be, and we must take care lest we forget that there are many things we need to talk about, to sort out. Serious theological conversation must accompany all our ecumenical ventures so that we might journey together closer to the Truth.

This was the Second Vatican Council, the opening of a door, and a very positive step. At the same time it is important to note that the Decree also teaches that the 'ecclesial Communities which are separated from us lack the fullness of unity with us flowing from Baptism ... we believe they have not retained the proper reality of the eucharistic mystery in its fullness, especially because of the absence of the sacrament of Orders' (*UR* 22). This question of an 'absence' of orders is a complex and sensitive issue, and is at the root of all questions concerning Eucharistic sharing. However, the concern of this chapter is the more immediate issue of intercommunion, or what might be termed 'communion in the meantime'.

Admission to Catholic Eucharistic Communion
Since the Second Vatican Council much has happened. In 1967 the Secretariat for Christian Unity, the body in Rome charged with ecumenical work, issued the first official post-Vatican II guidelines on intercommunion in its Directory on Ecumenism, *Ad Totam Ecclesiam*.[5] The document informs us that a separated baptised sister or brother (the term 'sister or brother' in itself indicates the recognition of relationship) was to be admitted to the Eucharist in a situation of urgent need (e.g. death, prison) providing the following four conditions were met:

1. The person has no access to a minister of their own communion;

2. Spontaneously asks for the sacraments;

3. Declares a faith in these sacraments in harmony with that of the Church;

4. And is rightly disposed.

A degree of authority was accorded to the diocesan bishop or the Episcopal Conference in decisions regarding 'urgent necessity', where it may not be quite as obvious as in the case of prison, or the proximity of death. This is quite remarkable. The Catholic Church will now sometimes permit other Christians to table fellowship. The discernment of 'urgent necessity', together with the statement that they must profess a faith 'in harmony' with that of the Church invite wise interpretation, and a listening to the Holy Spirit. 'Harmony' in faith refers to a belief in what Catholics term the Real Presence (see chapter seven). This belief is at the core of all conversations where Roman Catholics consider hospitality.

A document specifically addressing Eucharistic communion with other Christians was issued in 1972 again requiring a faith in 'conformity' with that of the Church, that is to say that the person professes a belief in the Real Presence.[6]

In 1993 a revision of the earlier directory was deemed necessary as ecumenical talks were progressing at a fast rate.[7] This document articulated clearly the foundations on which sacramental sharing is based. The Catholic Church understands all sacraments as acts of Christ and of the Church through the Spirit, simultaneously a sign of unity in faith, worship and community life, and a means for building this unity. While Catholics recognise the baptism of other Christian's as leading to what is termed 'a real, even if imperfect communion', to share the Eucharist normally requires full ecclesial communion (*Directory*, 129),[8] and so it is not possible to share eucharistic hospitality regularly with those who are in 'a real, even if imperfect communion'.

However, as has been the case since the Second Vatican Council, the *Directory* once more recognises that 'by way of exception, and under certain conditions', access to the Eucharist of non-Catholic Christians may be 'permitted, or even commended' (*Directory*, 129). The diocesan Bishop is normally the judge in these situations (*Directory*, 130). This increasing flexibility in the interpretation of the guidelines indicates growing sensitivity to different cultures, and a diversity of circumstances.

When it comes to the specific situation of 'mixed' marriages, intercommunion can be allowed in 'exceptional' circumstances. In the celebration of the sacrament of marriage itself, the diocesan Bishop may admit the non-Catholic partner to Eucharistic communion (*Directory*, 159), and during their time of marriage Eucharistic sharing may be permissible in 'exceptional' cases (*Directory*, 160). The term 'exceptional' allows a degree of latitude. Perhaps here again the criteria of a belief in harmony with that of the Catholic Church, that is to say a belief in the Real Presence, might allow for wide interpretation of the cases of 'exception'.

The next important development was John Paul II's Encyclical on Ecumenism, *Ut Unum Sint* (On Commitment to Ecumenism, May 1995), where he declared that 'it is a source of joy to note that Catholic ministers are able, in certain particular cases, to administer the Sacraments of the Eucharist, Penance and Anointing of the Sick to Christians who are not in full communion with the Catholic Church but who greatly desire to receive these sacraments, freely request them and manifest the faith which the Catholic Church professes with regard to these sacraments' (*Ut Unum Sint*, 46). The requirement that one does not have access to one's own minister has disappeared.

This is where teaching lies at the moment. It is at once clear and yet in need of interpretation by competent Episcopal bodies, and not least of wise pastoral application by ministers. The principle that the Eucharist is best understood as a visible expression of full visible union is held in creative tension with the desire for that union, and the realisation that 'exceptional' eucharistic sharing is permissible, due to our mutual recognition of the sacrament of baptism.

Another View

Before leaving this issue of communion sharing among Christians, from a Catholic perspective, it is helpful to listen to another perspective. In 1998 the Catholic Bishops of England, Wales, Scotland and Ireland issued a document entitled *One Bread, One Body*, teachings on the Eucharist and the issue of intercommunion.[9] This document, which reiterates the official Catholic Church's stance, at the same time recognising the pain of Christian disunity, of brokenness, and the need for reconciliation and healing (*One Bread, One Body*, 76-8), received a rigorous and insightful critique from Bishop Richard Clarke, the Church of Ireland Bishop of Kildare and Meath. This critique is a timely reminder that that which may seem 'open' and 'improved' from the insider's position (in this case the Roman Catholic Church), can be seen very differently by those whom it addresses.

Richard Clarke's study of the document is perceptive. Firstly he speaks of an unofficial 'pecking order' in the matter of Eucharistic sharing which, he remarks,

> might be comical if it were not tragic. The Orthodox Churches allow no other Christians to share sacramentally with them. The Roman Catholic Church would allow members of its church to receive the Orthodox sacraments were they permitted to do so by the Orthodox which they are not. Anglicans are, under their own rules, permitted to receive Roman Catholic or Orthodox sacraments, but we are permitted by neither to do so. And so on.[10]

It is indeed tragic. Clarke's response is to suggest that we need to distinguish between inter-communion, which can perhaps be too laissez-faire, and Eucharistic hospitality, which recognises that 'spiritual nourishment is always 'ecclesial'; it involves the visible community' (*One Bread, One Body*, 92). Most importantly, he reminds Christians that 'the Eucharist is not ours but Christ's, and that the invitation to receive the sacrament is ultimately his invitation not ours'. A sobering and challenging thought.

Perhaps we Roman Catholics need to be a little more humble in demanding that others hold the same Eucharistic faith as we do in order to share, in exceptional circumstances, communion with us. Indeed were we to explore the Eucharistic faith of all the Catholics gathered together on any given Sunday for Mass we would probably find a great diversity of belief. We don't, we cannot, understand what it is that we receive. The mystery is too great for our minds. Real Presence, transubstantiation, are all concepts that have been used to exclude, forgetting that in any use of these terms we are merely using words in an attempt to describe that which is beyond words. We need to be careful that we do not seek to over define what God does in the Eucharist. It is God's work, not ours.

Internal Church Questions
So it is God's work, we believe in the presence without really understanding this everyday miracle, and it is Christ who invites. Where does this leave us when we come to the question of those in 'irregular' relationships?

While there is a lot of debate on these issues, very little real fruitful discussion has taken place. The Church teaching is clear – those in 'irregular' relationships should not receive. The reality, and the pastoral response as we know, can often be different.

The German bishops have been particularly vocal in advocating a change in teaching with regard to those in second relationships. In this regard we might be able to learn from the Orthodox Church. Like the Roman Catholic Church, the Orthodox Church recognises marriage as a sacrament, yet at the same time it recognises that marriages breakdown for a multitude of reasons. Humans are frail and vulnerable, and God is merciful, loving. For this reason, the Orthodox Church, while reluctant, in certain circumstances permits a second, and even a third marriage, as a pastoral concession in the context of human weakness.

When it comes to other situations things are more complex, and yet one must ask if the norms of *Ut unum sint* might be applied in seeking to extend God's hospitality to these people. If those in 'irregular' relationships, a) freely desire to receive, b) freely request and c) manifest a faith which the Catholic Church professes with regard to the Eucharist, might they be permitted to receive? Perhaps this might be a more truthful witness to the

God of love? This is not to condone promiscuity, but advocates a belief in a 'bigger God', a God who 'saved us, not because of any works of righteousness that we had done, but according to God's mercy, through the water of rebirth and renewal by the Holy Spirit' (Titus 3:5). A God that continues to call Christians to greater maturity of decision making, and challenges us to consider deeply Richard Clarke's statement that 'the Eucharist is not ours but Christ's ... the invitation to receive the sacrament is ultimately his invitation not ours'.

A thought provoking scene in one of the Don Camillo films comes to mind.[11] Don Camillo, a priest in Italy post-World War II, is in continual conflict with Peppone, the major communist leader in the small town they live in. The situation is complex as it is Italian communism that is in question. One of the marks of the character of Dom Camillo are his frequent conversations with the figure of Jesus Christ on the crucifix. Don Camillo seeks advice and complains about the communists, especially Peppone, and Jesus frequently admonishes poor Don Camillo, continuously trying to teach him. In the relevant scene, Don Camillo refuses to baptise Peppone's baby, who has been brought by his mother and grandmother for baptism. Don Camillo, certain he is correct to refuse baptism to a communist's child, goes to Jesus for affirmation of his decision. Jesus' response is, as usual, unexpected: 'who are you Don Camillo to refuse baptism to this little child?' The Catholic question, while always aware of the precious gift entrusted to us, might thus become: 'who are we to refuse communion to this person?'

Perhaps we need to be slower to refuse, more willing to seek to educate people about the wondrous gift we have in the Eucharist, and to be more welcoming in the hope that all of us sinners will slowly become more like God through the reception of our daily bread. The Body of Christ is not limited to a consecrated host, it is organic, alive, growing, and groaning, seeking nourishment and love.

CHAPTER SIX

The Eucharist and Popular Devotions
'I am with you always' (Mt 28:20)

In the early days, as we have seen, Christians gathered together in one another's houses, shared a meal, and 'broke bread', in memory of the resurrected Lord. There was no church building, no altar, no tabernacle. The Eucharist was part of an ordinary meal. Probably because of abuses such as Paul talks about (1 Cor 11:17-34), a more stylised, ritualised way of giving thanks to God developed quite early on. While the idea of reserving the Blessed Sacrament for adoration, like we do today, was not yet in people's minds, there appears to have been a consistent belief in the enduring presence of Christ in the consecrated species. This we know as there are accounts of people bringing the consecrated bread home, for their own daily consumption, or to share with those who were not able to join the main assembly on Sunday. Justyn Martyr describes what happened in his community: the gifts 'over which the thanksgiving has been spoken are distributed, and everyone shares in them, while they are also sent via the deacons to the absent brethren' (*First Apology*, chapter 67). Thus, while we can say that reservation of the sacrament was a practice from the early days it was reserved for communion, for reception by those who could not attend the liturgy. Christians worshipped together, ate and drank together, prayed for those absent and ensured they were included in the 'eating', and perhaps even the 'drinking' of the Body and Blood of Christ.

The practices we have today with regard to reservation and adoration took a long time to develop, and while they are good and holy practices their beginning was often from what might be called the 'Eucharistic hunger' of the people deprived of a welcome to the Eucharistic table. 'Everyone shares in them', Justyn Martyr notes in the second century, however this changed quite quickly. It seems that from as early as the fourth and fifth centuries there was a decline in the number of people actually sharing, receiving communion (see chapter two). The reasons for this are difficult to know exactly. The address of a certain Abbot Theonas to some Egyptian monks, whom it seems were receiving only once a year is insightful:

> We ought not to suspend ourselves from the Lord's Communion because we confess ourselves sinners, but should more and more eagerly hasten to it for the healing of our soul, and purifying of our spirit, and seek there rather a remedy for our wounds with humility of mind and faith, as considering ourselves unworthy to receive so great grace. Otherwise we cannot worthily receive the Communion even once a year, as some do, who live in monasteries and so regard the dignity and holiness and value of the heavenly sacraments, as to think that none but saints and spotless persons should venture to receive them, and not rather that they would make us saints and pure by taking them. And these thereby fall into greater presumption and arrogance than what they seem to themselves to avoid, because at the time when they do receive them, they consider that they are worthy to receive them. But it is much better to receive them every Sunday for the healing of our infirmities, with that humility of heart, whereby we believe and confess that we can never touch those holy mysteries worthily, than to be puffed up by a foolish persuasion of heart, and believe that at the year's end we are worthy to receive them.
>
> John Cassian (c.360-c.435), *Conferences* 23:21

This teaching indicates that a sense of unworthiness played a part in people receiving less. Around this time too the development of a penitential discipline which excluded people from receiving communion would not have helped matters. The reasons for the increasing abstinence from communion were many and complex.[1]

True God and True Human

All this was probably enhanced by, and fed into, a very high Christology.[2] As people who had actually eaten and drunk with Jesus either before or after his resurrection, began to die, and as their children, the first generation to be told the story, began to die off, heresies and confusion abounded. The reality of the humanity of Jesus Christ was disputed, and an overemphasis on the divinity of Christ began to develop. This struggle in the Church to maintain a belief in Jesus Christ 'true God and true human' is one we will always have, because it is beyond our understanding. At different stages in history some people have stressed either Jesus' humanity, to the detriment of his divinity, or Christ's divinity, forgetting about his humanity. An early attempt to remind Christians of the true teaching was the Council of Chalcedon's declaration that:

> This selfsame one is perfect both in deity and in human-ness; this selfsame one is also actually God and actually human ... of the same reality as God as far as his deity is concerned and of the same reality as we ourselves as far as his humanness is concerned; thus like us in all respects, sin only excepted (*Definition of the Faith*, 451).

This is a constant doctrine of the Church needing to be safe-guarded; otherwise the risen Jesus too easily becomes a distant and unapproachable God, one no one could be worthy to receive.

However, despite this teaching, slowly but surely things changed and Jesus 'increased' in divinity in peoples' thought, and the liturgy of the Eucharist changed too. From being a remembrance of a meal that Jesus shared with his followers, the celebration of the Eucharist became a highly-ritualised and remote event, distanced from the everyday experience of peo-ple. This distancing was also reflected in the language. The lan-guage of the liturgy changed from Greek to Latin, the Church expanded, and many of the 'new' Christians did not understand the language of the liturgy. With the passage of time and expan-sion of the Church peoples' understanding of, and involvement in, the liturgy lessened. The priest and the sacrament became 'holier', the people gathered saw themselves increasingly as unworthy. This was a gradual process, taking place over a number of centuries, nevertheless slowly but surely eating and drinking at the Christian gathering was replaced by 'occular communion'; the desire to see the host replaced actual reception of the sacrament.

An Awesome Presence

These developments were also accompanied by controversies regarding how precisely Christ was present, and when precisely Christ became present.[3] Things came to a certain high point with the thought of a priest called Berengarius of Tours (999-1088), who publicly denied that Christ was really and physically present under the species of bread and wine. After much controversy, Pope Gregory VII became involved in the conflict and ordered Berengarius to sign a retraction. This statement, cited by Pope Paul VI in his *Mysterium Fidei* (1965), can be seen as the Church's first definitive statement regarding belief in the change of the bread and wine into the Body and Blood of Christ:

> I believe in my heart and openly profess that the bread and wine placed upon the altar are, by the mystery of the sacred prayer and the words of the Redeemer, substantially changed into the true and life-giving flesh and blood of Jesus Christ our Lord ...

While clarity was needed to respond to heretical positions, the impact of this clearer formulation of the reality of Christ's body in the Eucharist meant that 'the reception of that body became as awesome as it was full of promise'.[4] Increased awe and reverence lead to a fear of reception. That which they were invited to receive was so miraculous, so powerful, so awesome that unworthiness in the light of such great love crippled people in their sense of unworthiness, and so they received less and less. This sense of unworthiness also manifested itself in the practice of reception on the tongue for those of the laity who actually received. Their hands were unworthy to touch God. As fewer and fewer people received, the Eucharist came to be regarded as something to be looked at and adored, rather than something to be eaten and in a sense, changed into. The teaching of Pope Leo the Great (d.461) seems to have been forgotten:

For naught else is brought about by the partaking of the Body and Blood of Christ than that we pass into that which we then take, and both in spirit and in body carry everywhere Him, in and with Whom we were dead, buried, and rose again (*Sermon* 63).

Pope Leo's words fell on deafer and deafer ears. Visibility, seeing God, replaced communion with God and with one another. Rituals develop and the scene becomes wondrous. During the ninth century the practice of elevating of the host began. It seems to have developed as a gesture to enable people to see 'Christ's body'. Slowly but surely the moment(s) of elevation came to be seen as the high point of the Mass.[5] 'At the elevation all senses were called into play. Bells pealed, incense was burnt, candles were lit, hands clasped, supplications were mouthed.'[6] One can imagine the impact all this made on the senses of people who lived in a world without much else to stimulate them. The host was raised high so that people could adore and revere. This quickly became a centre of Eucharistic ritual action, and a way for people to express their love and reverence for the Eucharist, without actually receiving. Indeed stories abound of people running from church to church to see the host being elevated, and in this way to give glory to God. This development in sensual stimulation helped the liturgy to communicate with people at many levels, however the fact that less and less people were going to receive holy communion worried Church officials.

An official attempt to remedy the situation came with the Fourth Lateran Council's (1215) declaration making annual communion, preceded by confession, obligatory. Unfortunately, this teaching seems to have come to be regarded as one of sufficiency – it is enough to receive once a year – and so the practice of receiving just once a year became the norm for most people. This was the beginning of the practice of fulfilling 'one's Easter duty'.

From Justyn Martyr's picture of everyone sharing at the table of the Eucharist the practice has changed considerably. At the time of the Fourth Lateran Council, the priest was often the only one receiving at Mass. The Council encouraged communion at least once a year. A clear distinction between the priest, the cleric, and the rest of the people is being cemented. The development over time of canonical requirements such as distinct dress, celibacy, the requirement to pray the Divine Office of the Church, all add to this idea of difference. The priest came to be seen as holy, worthy to receive, while the congregation believed more and more strongly in their unworthiness, their great distance from God, and so they received less and less.[7]

Yet, even though people were not being encouraged to actively receive, they still wished to pray and adore. This shows the great love Christians have always had for the Eucharist. It is from this time of limited access to communion, from a great Eucharistic love, that the feast of Corpus Christi was born, as were the related practices of adoration and of benediction.

Corpus Christi

In many ways the celebration of Corpus Christi is 'the' Catholic feast. While some of our Anglican brothers and sisters also celebrate the feast with a procession, since the time of the Reformation it has come to be regarded as a mark of the Catholic faith, sometimes unhelpfully being used in a triumphal manner.[8] While today it might seem like the feast is going through a difficult phase, when we look back to its beginnings we see that it grew to universal prominence from very shaky beginnings. Liège in Belgium may be regarded as its birthplace. In the period of history with which we are concerned, the twelfth and thirteenth centuries, Liège was a prosperous centre of trade, and was also a great ecclesiastical centre. It was in this town, and in an era of Church history when visions and dreams were common and normally treated with great seriousness, that a woman, Juliana of Mont-Cornillon (1193-1258), had a vision regarded as foundational to the feast of Corpus Christi.[9]

According to an account in her life story, Julian had a Eucharistic vision in which she saw the full moon, which had a segment darkened with a blemish.

> I tell you that a moon appeared to her in its splendour, with a little break in part of its sphere. She watched this for a long while, wondered a lot, and did not know what this might portend.[10]

Some twenty years later this dream was repeated and according to the story, its meaning revealed by Christ himself:

> Then Christ revealed to her that the Church was in the moon, and that the missing part of the moon stood for the absence of one feast in the Church, which he would want his faithful to celebrate on earth.[11]

For many years she kept her dream secret, only revealing it some years later to her confessor John of Lausanne, who spoke about it publicly. That someone should have a dream about the Eucharist in Liège was not surprising. This area was so famous for its devotion to the Eucharist that St Francis is said to have deemed it a suitable venue for his order because the people here 'show greatest reverence for the Body of Christ' (*Scripta Leonis*, 79, 226-7).

Juliana's visions took place in a receptive atmosphere and gave weight to her desire, shared by many others, for the institution of a Eucharistic feast, in response to Christ's request. The local bishop Robert of Turotte was supportive and established a feast of the Eucharist in his diocese through his pastoral letter *Inter alia mira* (1246). The first 'feast of the Sacrament' as it was initially known, *Corpus Christi*, took place in 1246. It was a local feast, and could easily have died out as Bishop Robert died shortly afterwards, and the next bishop was not so supportive of Juliana.

However all was not lost. Jacques Pantaleon, an archdeacon in Liège (1243-8), was present at the feast's foundation in 1246, and on 27 August 1261 he became Pope Urban IV. The feast had now gained support in high places. In August 1264 Urban IV established *Corpus Christi* as a universal feast to be celebrated on the Thursday following Trinity Sunday. He is also reputed to have requested Thomas Aquinas to compose the Divine Office for this feast day.[12]

The death of Pope Urban IV a few months later once more made the future of the feast precarious. However at the Council of Vienne (1311), Pope Clement V promoted *Corpus Christi* and his successor Pope John XXII continued to urge its observance. It quickly grew, and a procession became part of the celebration, perhaps the most popular part of it. Today *Corpus Christi* continues to be an important feast of the Church, and while the number and the size of the processions may have reduced in places, the feast still serves to remind us that as Christ promised, he is with us.

Forty Hours

Another great Eucharistic devotion, though a popular rather than an official one, is that of the Forty Hours (*Quarant' Ore*) of continuous prayer made before the exposed Blessed Sacrament. No one is clear about the origins of this devotion but there are accounts of a Forty Hours taking place in Italy, in Milan in 1537. It must have been quite remarkable because the devotions took place in all the churches in Milan, one after the other, keeping the devotion going, thus ensuring continual prayer was maintained in the city before the exposed Blessed Sacrament. The aim, it seems, was to pray continuously and publicly to keep Milan Christians safe from the many perils surrounding them. Charles Borromeo (1538-1584), Archbishop of Milan, a key figure in the reform of the Church in the years after the Council of Trent, is reputed to have claimed the practice as a very ancient one. He is the one said to have made the link between the forty hours Jesus spent in the tomb, this forty hours that his followers had waiting, in prayer, before the resurrection, to the practice he was promoting of the forty hours of prayer before the Blessed Sacrament.

In 1731 Pope Clement XII wrote a document giving detailed guidelines for adoration. It gave instructions for such things as the number of candles to be used, the incensing of the Blessed Sacrament and the decoration of the altar. The document also prohibited the ringing of bells during exposition. All this was done to ensure a 'special' prayerful atmosphere could be 'felt' in the church during the Forty Hours. Peoples' senses were being 'spoken' to. It is in these instructions that the rituals for Benediction find their roots.

Benediction

Benediction of the Blessed Sacrament consists of a solemn service of prayer, in which the Blessed Sacrament is exposed on the altar in a monstrance (a receptacle, usually of gold or silver, which has a transparent part in which the consecrated Host is placed for adoration). The monstrance is surrounded by candles. Hymns, including the *Tantum Ergo*, composed by Thomas Aquinas for *Corpus Christi*, are sung and prayers are recited. The incensing of the Blessed Sacrament is also a part of the prayer in Ireland. At the end of the service the priest takes the monstrance, lifts it and with it makes the sign of the cross, in silence, over the kneeling congregation. This is where the name Benediction comes from (from the Latin word, *benedicare* meaning to wish well, to bless).

Adoration

Linked to these practices is that of prayer before the Blessed Sacrament, whereby people are encouraged to visit the church and pray in the presence of the Blessed Sacrament, reserved in a tabernacle, and the practice of adoration, when the Blessed Sacrament is exposed, placed in a monstrance on the altar, for people to pray before. What is termed Perpetual Adoration is a particular form of adoration before the exposed Blessed Sacrament. In this form of prayer a parish or a religious community arrange for continual exposition where someone is always present in prayer before the Blessed Sacrament. While all these practices are good and holy, the Congregation for Divine Worship in Rome remind us to vigilantly ensure that all Eucharistic worship which takes place outside of the actual celebration of the eucharistic liturgy is ordered to it (*The Year of the Eucharist: Suggestions and Proposals*, 2004).

Eucharistic Congress

Another, more recent expression of eucharistic devotion, is the holding of Eucharistic Congresses. According to a Vatican website, Eucharistic Congresses aim to increase 'understanding and participation in the Eucharistic Mystery in all its aspects: from the celebration to worship *extra missam* (outside of Mass), so that its influence permeates the whole of personal and social life'. A Eucharistic Congress is a call to live more eucharistically and the essentials of a Congress are identified as prayer in common, adoration of the Blessed Sacrament, eucharistic processions, and of course the celebration of the Eucharist itself.

Eucharistic Congresses are a relatively new practice in the history of the Church, 'born' from the eucharistic apostolate of

Saint Peter-Julian Eymard (1811-1868), a Frenchman, and from
Émilie-Marie Tamisier's (1834-1910) ideas on 'eucharistic
pilgrimages'.[13] The first congress, a local event, was held in
Lille, France in 1881. Each year since then the idea has steadily
grown, and the event has become international. From its earliest
days the idea of Eucharist as a call to action has been promoted
with time being allocated at Reims (1894) for a study of social
questions affecting the working classes and in Angers (1901) for
a discussion of papers concerning social questions. It was also
after the 1905 Congress, held in Rome, that Pope Pius X issued
his teaching advising people to receive daily communion
(*Tridentina Synodus*, 20 December, 1905), thus recognising the
centrality of Eucharist for all. 'Ocular' communion is not
enough. A few years later the Decree *Quam Singulari* (Sacred
Congregation for the Sacraments, 8 August 1910) permitted
children to receive Holy Communion once they could tell the
difference between communion bread and ordinary bread.
Seven years was suggested, a much younger age than the previ-
ous practice of receiving one's first Holy Communion at the age
of ten, twelve, or even older. With these changes in teaching
Pius X was reminding the Church that the Eucharist is food for
the vulnerable and the weak, for all of us, to sustain us on our
life journey, and to help us to grow into holiness. His teachings
were attempts to encourage the Church to return to receiving
regularly. At the same time they also remind us that the
Eucharist is a mystery which shall never be fathomed, in this
way warning against too precise formulations.

While today (twenty-first century) Benediction and the Forty
Hours are less popular than previously, the practice of adoration of the Blessed Sacrament remains a popular devotion in the
Catholic Church. All this is good as these practices remind us of
the enduring presence of Christ with us, and they help us to stay
in prayer with God. It is essential that this way of prayer maintain a close connection with its source, the celebration of the
liturgy of the Eucharist, the Mass. Time spent with the Lord in
adoration, and time spent with our community celebrating the
great gift of Emmanuel, God-with-us, must gradually transform
us so that we slowly but surely become divinised, and seek to
divinise the world.

CHAPTER SEVEN

Some Theological Thoughts

'Faith and reason are like two wings on which the
human spirit rises to the contemplation of truth'
(Pope John Paul II)[1]

While the mystery of the Eucharist is well beyond our compre-
hension, this does not mean that we should leave our minds
behind when we come to celebrate Eucharist. Human beings
have been gifted with very great intellects. While we are like
other animals in many ways, we are radically distinct from
them because we can think and question and can really come to
know God. We can enter into relationship with God, or we can
choose not to relate with God, to reject God's offer of friendship.
The fact that we think and reason is evidenced by the number of
books that have been printed over the years on this greatest of
mysteries: the Eucharist. In human attempts to talk about
Eucharist, new words like transubstantiation have been bor-
rowed from the world of philosophy, and old words, such as
'sacrifice' have been used in new ways. This chapter shall try to
explain these theological ideas in a way that 'makes sense'.
These are not dry words used by theologians who seek to take
from the mystery being celebrated, but words which make a
difference, words which, as the theologian Herbert McCabe
says, 'crack open as we use them to reach towards God'.

Transubstantiation
Firstly, transubstantiation, a word that has caused many problems over the ages. So often people are heard to say things such
as, 'We (Catholics) believe in transubstantiation, Protestants
don't.' Care is needed as things are not quite as simple or as
straightforward as this. The word is one thing, the meaning it
seeks to communicate is another.

As was said earlier (chapter four), the word transubstantiation was first used in the Middle Ages. Up to then it seems that

people were happy enough to pray the Eucharist, and to share the consecrated bread and the consecrated wine. They believed in the Real Presence, but they were not overly concerned about what happened, about how bread and wine became Body and Blood. It was in the ninth century that the debates began in earnest. Some people emphasised a very physical presence, claiming they were actually eating Christ's flesh. At the other extreme people stressed that the presence was spiritual, symbolic. It proved very difficult to put what happens into words. No word can ever properly describe it. One might say that each time we gather and pray the Eucharist a miracle takes place. We ask God to send the Holy Spirit to change physical material, perishable things, into spiritual imperishable nourishment. The term used to describe this calling on, this invocation of the Holy Spirit, is the *epiclesis*. In the Fourth Eucharistic Prayer we pray: 'may this same Holy Spirit graciously sanctify these offerings'. During the Middle Ages some people started to use the word 'transubstantiation' to describe the change effected by the Holy Spirit.

The decision of the Dominican theologian St Thomas Aquinas (c.1225 – 1274) to use this word in his writings ensured that the term 'transubstantiation' became central to Catholic teaching. The change that he sought to describe was mysterious, a change like no other that we know of in this world, and for this reason he knew that a 'new' word, from outside of theology was needed. This change of bread and wine into the Body and Blood of Christ needed a special word, a term of its own, and so Thomas said 'it can be called transubstantiation'.[2] Thomas did not seek to define, or limit what happened, nor have any of the teachings of the Church since, but the Church leadership has, despite many arguments and controversies decided to stick with this term as they know that no term will ever be adequate.[3] It is a miracle.

The term simply and yet most profoundly asserts the Real Presence of Jesus Christ in the consecrated species. The Council of Trent (1545-1563), held in response to the Reformation in an attempt to give clarity to Roman Catholic Church teaching, explains what it understood was happening:

the holy Synod teaches, and openly and simply professes, that, in the august sacrament of the holy Eucharist, after the consecration of the bread and wine, our Lord Jesus Christ, true God and human, is truly, really, and substantially contained under the species of those sensible things … sacramentally present to us in his own substance, by a manner of existing, which, though we can scarcely express it in words, yet can we, by the understanding illuminated by faith, conceive, and we ought most firmly to believe, to be possible unto God (Council of Trent, *Thirteenth Session*, chapter une).

While this might sound like a jungle of archaic words, it is saying something very important: Christ is really present, substantially, sacramentally, in a manner 'we can scarcely express'. We are in the world of mystery. The Real Presence is a matter of faith. It looks like bread, it tastes like wine, and yet Christ is substantially present. Archaic though they may be, words are of great importance. Following the teaching of Thomas Aquinas, Trent teaches us that the most appropriate (Latin, *aptissime*, most apt) way to speak about this change is by using the term transubstantiation.[4] It doesn't say this is the only way, nor does it claim that we can now define what happens. The decision to use this word transubstantiation is a way of continually reminding us that we are trying to talk about a mystery, an indescribable mystery. To put an end to dispute and controversy the Council of Trent invites Catholics to settle on a word, 'transubstantiation', aware that no word will ever be good enough. Many other Christians believe in a 'change' of the bread and wine which results in a Real Presence of Jesus the Christ, the Risen Lord.[5] Catholics have chosen to settle on the term transubstantiation to describe this change.

Sometimes we are tempted to think of a moment of change, a particular time of the Mass when transubstantiation occurs. While Trent might be read as saying this, its main concern is to teach of the Real Presence, to reaffirm that the whole Christ is truly, really, and substantially contained in the Eucharistic species. More recent Catholic theology, especially since the Second Vatican Council has emphasised the unity of the

Eucharistic prayer. Since the Eucharistic Prayer is a whole, a unity, it is as a whole that it possesses an *epicletic* nature.[6] The whole prayer is an invocation of the Holy Spirit. This teaching

> says something about the nature of the Church and the sacraments. The sacraments are not simply an extension of the person and work of Jesus Christ in the sphere of the Church; the Church must, rather, ask for the Spirit so as to recall Jesus Christ and His saving work. The Church has, in overall terms, an epicletic structure. It does not 'have' the Holy Spirit nor is the Holy Spirit at the disposal of the Church. However, it can and may ask for the coming of the Holy Spirit and can be certain that this plea will be heard.[7]

What is perhaps even more radical, and less often proclaimed, is that just as bread and wine are offered to God we too offer ourselves up to God, we pray that we too might be transformed into the Body and Blood of Christ. We plead with the Holy Spirit to also ensure worthy and fruitful reception of the sacrament of the Eucharist. This is the Christian call. We do not only offer up our daily work, our money, our prayers to God: God asks nothing less than all from each one of us. We have been baptised into the life, death and resurrection of Jesus. We are called to live differently, to live as Christians in the world. We have been created after the image and likeness of God and we are invited to grow daily into that image. This is impossible alone, or by our own efforts. For this reason we come together regularly, weekly, daily or occasionally to pray that this might happen. We pray that slowly we too may become 'transubstantiated' into the Body and Blood of Christ. We are the Body of Christ.

In a sense two miracles take place at each celebration of the Eucharist. The body of Christ is made present sacramentally, substantially, by God's word through the power of the Holy Spirit. What happens next though is perhaps even more of a mystery. Before we actually receive the consecrated bread and wine, the minister proclaims the truth that this is 'the Body of Christ', the 'Blood of Christ'. We answer with the simple term

'Amen'. This is the deepest prayer we can offer. It simply means 'I believe', 'I agree', 'I assent'. 'Amen, yes I believe in the presence of Jesus the Christ, the Risen Lord, in the consecrated elements, bread and wine.' 'I believe in the presence of Christ sacramentally in Holy Communion.' In faith we believe that this bread and wine are no longer ordinary bread and wine, they have been changed at their deepest level, in their meaning, in what they mean for us. They are no longer ordinary food and drink but they have now become for us food for eternal life. For this reason, to partake in the sacrament of the Eucharist, to eat the bread and drink the wine, is no small act for a Christian. It is a concrete statement of who we are, and who we are to become. We are good, and we will become 'godly', divinised, deified. We too, one might say, become 'transubstantiated'. Augustine puts it well:

> Love knows it. O Eternal Truth, and true Love, and loved Eternity! You are my God ... as if I heard this voice of Yours from on high: 'I am the food of strong people; grow, and you shall feed upon me; nor shall you convert me, like the food of your flesh, into you, but you shall be converted into me' (Augustine *Confessions*, Book 7.10.16).

Sacrifice

> I myself ... say that prayers and thanksgiving made by worthy persons are the only sacrifices that are perfect and well-pleasing to God (Justyn Martyr, *Dialogue with Trypho the Jew*, 117.2).

It seems very strange to speak of the Mass as sacrifice. For the first few hundred years Christians did not think of their gatherings to break bread as like the sacrifices of pagans, and they were right, yet why did the Second Vatican Council decide to stress again the sacrificial aspect of the Eucharist? Again, here we find God turning things upside down, changing our understanding of words. The Mass is indeed a sacrifice, but it is sacrifice in a radically different way to the traditional understanding of sacrifice. We might speak about making sacrifices so we can save up money to send our children to college, or so that we can go on a holiday. People often talk about making a sacrifice for Lent, giving up something, sweets or alcohol or maybe coffee. We give up something we really like, to 'discipline' ourselves, or to offer it up to God for our sins – whatever that might mean.

This type of understanding of sacrifice is a very ancient one. In the past, and in some places today, the offering of sacrifice was central to peoples and their religions. Normally an animal, a blood sacrifice was offered to placate the god, to keep the god happy, or to 'pay' the god for something we are asking the god to do. The priest, the intermediary between the god(s) and the rest of the people, offers the sacrifice. Afterwards there was often feasting, where the sacrificed animal was eaten, and singing and dancing to thank the god for doing whatever it was we had asked for – a good harvest, protection from the enemy, or cures from illnesses. In this society, the priest, the intermediary is very important. He has the power to communicate with the god. The god is usually seen as rather distant, and vengeful. If we don't offer sacrifice to placate the god, or gods, something dreadful might happen to us.

Over time the Jewish people moved from this type of thinking and came to see that their God was not like other gods, their God did not need to be appeased, or be sacrificed to in the hope of a good harvest. They came to see that their God was radically different and wanted no bloody sacrifice: 'I desire steadfast love and not sacrifice, the knowledge of God rather than burnt-offerings' (Hos 6:6). The God the Jewish people came to know simply wanted worship and thanksgiving and so they slowly came to see themselves as a priestly people (Ex 19:5-6). As a priestly people they would offer prayers of praise and thanksgiving to God on behalf of all humankind. They, the people, understood that they replaced the sacrificing priest and so their whole understanding of God underwent a radical revision.[8]

The early Christians, many of whom were Jewish-Christians, developed this way of thinking. They did not see Jesus' death on the cross as something which took place to calm a god angry at a sinful people. It was not the 'father' sacrificing his 'son' in a most horrendous fashion. In the story we gather to commemorate, the Paschal Mystery, we hear over and over again the story of the rejection of goodness and love. Jesus, God incarnate, is goodness and love made flesh. Our ancestors were unable to accept the challenge goodness posed, and Jesus did not resist them when they came to arrest and crucify him. Jesus, the priest, offered his very self as the victim. For Christians it is Christ himself who provides the sacrificial meal (See *Catechism of the Catholic Church*, n. 1365). It is the priest become offering that we feast on, and in this way we slowly become a priestly people.

> Come to him, a living stone, though rejected by mortals yet chosen and precious in God's sight, and like living stones, let yourselves be built into a spiritual house, to be a holy priesthood, to offer spiritual sacrifices acceptable to God through Jesus Christ (1 Pet 2:4-5).

When we gather to celebrate the sacrificial meal of the Eucharist we are in solidarity with Christ on the cross. We, the people, are the priesthood offering the sacrifice ... through Jesus Christ. When we gather to celebrate the sacrament of the Eucharist, to partake of the Eucharistic sacrifice, we are commemorating, remembering our baptism into Christ, into the life, death and resurrection of Christ. We have been baptised into the Body of Christ, the Holy Spirit has been breathed upon us, and so when we gather together to pray we really are Christ praying, and Christ offering his sacrifice. We do not re-sacrifice, re-crucify Christ but we enter into the eternal now of 'God's time', which is outside of time, and we remember what happened as if we were there (*anamnesis*) – we are there, on the cross, at the foot of the cross, and through this remembering we enter into solidarity with all humankind, especially with suffering humankind.

The role of the presider, the ordained priest is crucial. It is a continual reminder of the Catholic nature of our Church.

> At Mass we all consecrate the bread and wine through the ministry of the priest. He is there to represent our priesthood. And, in doing so, he does not just represent the congregation present with him. He represents the baptismal priesthood of the whole Church throughout the world. The presiding priest is consecrated by the whole Church to represent the whole Church; he is there

because we are not simply a local group of Christians praying. We are the whole Church praying. So we are Christ praying, Christ offering his sacrifice, Christ handing himself over to us in the form of food and drink, Christ providing the sacrificial meal in which we show our solidarity with each other and with all victims of this world: the sacrificial meal in which we are in solidarity with the victim on the cross through whom all humankind is brought through death and out of death to unity in the eternal life of love.[9]

This way of thinking of the Mass as sacrifice, recovered at the Second Vatican Council, reminds us that to speak of eucharistic sacrifice is primarily to speak of Christ's presence among us, Christ's salvific, saving presence. 'The Eucharist is thus a sacrifice because it re-presents (makes present) the sacrifice of the cross, because it is its memorial and because it applies its fruit'(*Catechism of the Catholic Church*, n.1366). It is through the story of Christ's death and resurrection that salvation is gifted to us. Christ did not have to 'pay' God back for our sins, to make 'restitution' for our shortcomings.[10] In the story of the cross we see that God's response to the greatest sin ever, the crucifixion of love on the cross, is resurrection, forgiveness, the rebirth of hope, a new covenant. The understanding of sacrifice is changed.

This is what we remember each time we gather to pray the Mass. We hear what Jesus did and what God has done, and is doing, for us in Jesus. We enter God's 'time' which is outside of created time. Just as Jesus once historically, put himself at the disposal of human judgement, placing his vulnerability as a human in the hands of our ancestors – this is what he does, in a sense, each time we receive communion. We gather and remember that 'we' crucified him because we could not accept his great goodness and love, his practice of table fellowship which threatened, and threatens, our security so much. We did not know what we were doing (Lk 23:34). God's response to Jesus' death on a cross was the Resurrection. God said 'no' to the greatest sin of the world, the crucifixion of his Son, love incarnate, on a cross. Today little has changed. We continue to struggle to live as lovingly as we should, we prey on vulnerability, we sin. God's response has not changed either. To a people at once sinful and holy, God says, 'take and eat'. The choice is ours. This is justice in a Godly, not worldly, way.

The sacrifice on the cross, marks the beginning of the new covenant that God is making with humankind. This new covenant represents a new vision of God. This covenant is ratified not by the fact of the suffering and the death on the cross but by an act of love. Jesus freely accepted his horrendous death on a cross. He freely accepted it because he loved us, he loved us enough to suffer the fate that always meets real love in our world.

In the Shadow of the Cross

This is the story of each Eucharistic gathering. We remind ourselves of what God has done for us, and we remind God, and we beseech God, 'Look, you have rescued us before, you have never yet abandoned us, please do not abandon us now.' The story tells us that God has always cared for us, so we believe in faith that God will always care for us. We believe, in trust, that we too will be 'transubstantiated' by the power of the Holy Spirit through our regular participation in the ritual retelling of the story, the Eucharist. The story of the death and resurrection of Jesus is the greatest account of God's covenantal, ever present care. When we eat together, we do so in anticipation of the future life of glory with God, but we eat and drink always under the shadow of the cross. This image is always kept before our eyes – we Catholics generally use a crucifix to remind us continuously of the reality of the suffering that Jesus endured for our salvation. We keep this image of the crucified Lord always before our eyes as he is the source of our life and salvation. It is in the shadow of the crucifix that we gather to celebrate the Eucharist, to give thanks for the death on the cross and the resurrection from the dead. Both are important to our faith. And in the shadow of this cross is precisely where we see love manifest. Love is what led Jesus to the cross.[11]

CHAPTER EIGHT

The Eucharistic Vocation
'Go, glorify the Lord by your life'

The Eucharist then is sacrifice and sacrament, it is the great prayer of the Church, it is 'the source and summit of the Christian life'(*LG* 11). Through the prayers and readings of our Eucharistic gathering we are plunged, yet again, into the whole story of God's saving presence in human history, a presence which led to the incarnation, Immanuel, God is with us. The Paschal Mystery, the story of Jesus' death and resurrection, speaks of the mystery of God's continuing presence among us. This Christ who is risen from the dead, is the one who showed his hands and his sides to his followers, and said: 'Peace be with you. As the Father has sent me, so I send you.' When he had said this, he breathed on them and said to them, 'Receive the Holy Spirit' (Jn 20:21-22). In every Eucharistic gathering Jesus breathes the Holy Spirit on each one of us, and sends us forth, to live as he lived. This is a remarkable claim, and one that we can only fulfil in the power of the Spirit.

Go Forth in the Power of the Spirit
The message, the Christian vocation, is clear. To follow Jesus the Christ is about a lot more than going to Mass, it is to be sent into the world, transformed by the power of the Holy Spirit ('transubstantiated'), to spread the good news of salvation everywhere. There is a particular way of life that Christians are called to: 'Blessed are those who hunger and thirst for righteousness … Blessed are the merciful, for they will receive mercy … Blessed are the peacemakers, for they will be called children of God' (Mt 5:6-9). Those who claim to follow Jesus must seek to live as he did. To become a Christian is a life long journey. It begins with our baptism, when we are baptised into the story of Jesus, immersed into his life and death, and is continually nourished through our celebration of the Eucharist. Each Eucharist we

attend ends with the words, '*Ite, missa est*'. Read literally this is simply a dismissal, go, the Mass is over. From the earliest days Christians came to see this sending as a command to go forth, in the power of the Spirit, to proclaim the Good News of the Gospel to the world. All baptised people are called to live the missionary call of the Church. We are told to 'go' but to go and do something. The words of Dismissal reflect this:

Go forth, the Mass is ended.
Go and announce the Gospel of the Lord.
Go in peace, glorifying the Lord by your life.
Go in peace.

We are to 'go forth' to 'announce the Gospel of the Lord', we are to glorify the Lord by the very living of our lives. In 2007 Pope Benedict XVI wrote a document on the Eucharist, *Sacramentum Caritatis*, the Sacrament of Love, and in it he described the dismissal as a starting-point to the Church's life (*Sacramentum Caritatis*, 51). It is essential, he said, that we, the People of God, be missionary. It is not a choice. Catholics are indeed called to gather and celebrate Eucharist but the vocation of a Catholic is at once a call to live differently in the world, to live eucharistically. Whenever we fail to do this a shadow is cast over our liturgical practice. Our prayer becomes untruthful. The Christian philosopher Nicholas Wolterstorff starkly claims that 'liturgy practiced in the absence of justice is so seriously mal-formed that God finds it disgusting'.[1]

The Most Precious Temple of All
These are strong words, but they claim nothing new. It has always been the Church's position. St John Chrysostom's homily reminds us of the essential link between the Eucharist and our neighbour:

Do you want to honour Christ's body? Then do not scorn him in his nakedness, nor honour him here in the church with silken garments while neglecting him outside where he is cold and naked. For he who said: This is my body, and made it so by his words, also said: 'You saw me hungry and did not feed me, and inasmuch as you did not do it for one of these, the least of my brothers or sisters, you did not do it for me' (Mt 25:34ff). What we do here in the church requires a pure heart, not special garments; what we do outside requires great dedication …

For God does not want golden vessels but golden hearts.

No one has ever been accused for not providing ornaments (for the church), but for those who neglect their neighbour a hell awaits with an inextinguishable fire and torment in the company of the demons. Do not, therefore, adorn the church and ignore your afflicted brother or sister, for he or she is the most precious temple of all (St John Chrysostom, *Gospel of Matthew*, Homily 50).

These are indeed beautiful, challenging words. God wants golden hearts, our afflicted sister or brother is the most precious temple of all. If we can provide a beautiful dwelling for the consecrated species, for the Real Presence in the consecrated host, we are challenged to do this also for our neighbour. It is not too difficult to be reverent toward the host, but we are challenged to grow in reverence for our neighbour, who is also a dwelling place of God, a 'tabernacle'.

The Ten Commandments given to Moses are summarised very clearly by Jesus. Christians who wish to inherit eternal life are called to 'love the Lord your God with all your heart, and with all your soul, and with all your strength, and with all your mind; and your neighbour as yourself' (Lk 10:27). The three go together. Theologians will often speak of the horizontal and vertical sides to our faith. The vertical means our relationship with God. This we practice most especially when we gather to pray the Eucharist together, and indeed whenever we pray, or read scriptures, or read other good spiritual and theological books. The horizontal part of faith must accompany this. This is our mission to the world. We are to care for our sisters and brothers.

We are all part of the Body of Christ, this is what we proclaim each time we say *Amen*, and in a particularly powerful way as we receive communion. When one part of the Body is sick or ill or suffering we have a responsibility to care, to listen, to help in whatever way we can. This is Catholic doctrine, this is what

Catholics are called to do, to live lives in memory of Christ. Each Eucharist we share must show itself to be in harmony with the many meals Jesus shared with all sorts of people. Jesus gave his life 'for the life of the world' (Jn 6:51). The Catholic call is to serve the world, to give our lives for the world. The table fellowship we share with other Catholics is to become a fellowship shared with all, especially those in need.

The gospels speak to us of Jesus' deep compassion for everyone, especially for the suffering and for sinners (Mt 20:34; Mk 6:34; Lk 19:41). The Eucharist is a sacramental reminder of God's compassion towards all our brothers and sisters, not just the baptised. My sharing in the eucharistic mystery impels me toward a life of charity. Through constant schooling in the Eucharistic mystery, the regular breathing of the Holy Spirit into the depth of my being, I slowly learn to 'love even the person whom I do not like or even know ... I learn to look on this other person not simply with my eyes and my feelings, but from the perspective of Jesus Christ' (*Sacramentum Caritatis*, 88).

The Food of Truth

This is indeed a challenge but it is the Christian call. Jesus' meals were a prophetic sign to us of this call. His meals were probably an uncomfortable place for many, forced to eat with those they would prefer not to, or else simply looking on, observing, and wondering what was going on. Feeding the neighbour I see is a starting point, but seeking to live eucharistically is not a mere call to be concerned about my neighbour but it is a call to social action, toward courageous action here and now. The writings of Pope Benedict in his document on the Eucharist, leave us in no doubt:

> Precisely because of the mystery we celebrate, we must denounce situations contrary to human dignity, since Christ shed his blood for all, and at the same time affirm the inestimable value of each individual person (*Sacramentum Caritatis*, 89).

The Eucharist is the Food of Truth. The Catholic is called to learn to see the truth, to open our eyes to the injustices in the world and to try to do something about them. Like the disciples of old we must pray so that we might be filled with the Holy Spirit and proclaim God's word of truth with boldness (Acts 4:31).

The call to live the truth in love has many aspects. It may demand of us that we join organizations that campaign against injustice, and call for change. We need to learn to see unjust structures and seek to work for their transformation. Sometimes this call to truth, to see more truthfully and to 'do justice'[2] may be much nearer home, and thus more difficult to act upon. There may be injustices in my workplace, in my home, and of course we are also called to open our eyes to injustices in our Church.

The hunger for the Eucharist might be one such injustice. Many Catholics hunger for weekly Eucharist, some because they have no access to an ordained minister, others because teachings deem that they should not share communion with the Eucharistic gathering. In his address to the Bishops' Synod on the Eucharist (2005) John Atcherley Dew, the Archbishop of Wellington, acutely aware of this fact, reminds us to,

> look for ways to include those who are hungering for the Bread of Life. The scandal of the hungering for eucharistic food needs to be addressed, just as the scandal of physical hunger needs to be addressed.

The Church is a Church of saints and of sinners, we are an *'ecclesia semper reformanda'*, a Church always in need of reform.

Care for Creation

The horizontal dimension of the Christian eucharistic vocation is also a call to respect, and protect creation. The call to *Eucharistia*, to give thanks to God for the gift of salvation is no less a call to give thanks to God for creation. In recent years we have become aware of how intimately linked with our eucharistic vocation is the call to care for creation. God has created all that is, and so creation is good. The 'fruit of the vine' and the 'work of human hands' that we offer to God in our eucharistic liturgies is symbolic of all of creation. We give thanks through the Eucharist for the goodness of creation, a creation through which God reveals Godself to the world. The Christian story teaches that the world is not some indifferent raw material for human kind to dominate and use selfishly, solely for our own purposes. The world, and all that is in it, is a gift to be used well for the sake of all. When I use water, or my car, there is an effect on the environment we all share. Perhaps one of the most important truths that we have come to see more clearly in recent decades is the recognition that the Christian vocation is a vocation to be 'green'. To live eucharistically means that Christians are compelled to respond to the threat to the environment and to 'working responsibly for the protection of creation' (*Sacramentum Caritatis*, 92).

Communion of Saints

Every time Catholics assemble to celebrate the Eucharist we congregate conscious that when we gather we pray not only for those gathered in this church today, but for the whole world (Eucharistic Prayer IV: 'remember now all for whom we offer this sacrifice … those gathered here before you, your entire people, and all who seek you with a sincere heart.'). We pray conscious that we are part of something much bigger than what we can see, we are part of what the Catholic Church teaches is the communion of saints. The communion of saints is a solidarity of all peoples, living and dead. We believe that we can pray for our dead, and that they pray for us. This relationship continually reminds us that death is not the end. We are destined for eternal life with God, and with the saints who have gone before us. As well as the communion of saints the Catholic Church also speaks of a communion in holy things (*Catechism of the Catholic Church*, n. 948). We the holy people, the communion of saints gathered in the church are fed by holy things, the Body and Blood of Christ, so that we might grow in holiness. We are fed, the Holy Spirit breathed upon us, so that we might become agents of holiness and hope in the world. We are fed so that when we get to heaven we will be 'full' of holiness. We will be deified. In a sense while we enjoy the foretaste of the heavenly banquet here, we are eating and drinking our way to heaven at each eucharistic gathering.

To Live Well

This regular nourishment by the Eucharist is gift and responsibility. The gift enables us to live our responsibilities well. The responsibilities, as Jesus outlined them, are to God, and to our neighbour. The responsibility to our neighbour includes the responsibility for our environment, the world my neighbour inhabits. One responsibility that can sometimes be forgotten about is the responsibility to myself. Jesus' command is to 'love my neighbour as myself'. To love myself, this is indeed a challenge. How to love myself rightly, justly and with mercy, is a life time vocation, and one often forgotten about, and rarely preached. Indeed the media and advertising invite me to 'love' myself but they seem to send me in strange directions. Chocolate bars, expensive cars, the perfect partner and designer clothes all promise happiness, but really cause me to desire more and more of things that will not ultimately help me to live better as a Christian. They will not help me to become holy. Jesus' words to the Pharisees are more helpful: 'Go and learn what this means, "I desire mercy, and not sacrifice." For I came not to call the righteous, but sinners'(Mt 9:13). We are safe, Jesus came to call sinners, and we are invited to learn the practice of mercy. Regular participation in the Eucharist provides us with this schooling in mercy. The Holy Spirit is the teacher (Jn 14:26). The task is to learn to be merciful to ourselves so that we can share this mercy with others. Perhaps this is the essential message of the Eucharist, the one that encapsulates much of its great richness. The Eucharist we celebrate is a celebration of the great mercy of God. God forgave us for crucifying his Son. God was merciful, God is merciful, God will be merciful.

A Taste of Heaven

The Eucharist is also called food for the journey, *viaticum*. The journey is the journey toward God, *viaticum* the name traditionally used to describe the Eucharist when we share it with someone who is sick or dying. We are all on the journey toward God, and there we believe and trust that we shall meet a God of mercy. Jesus Christ, we pray will be our merciful judge.

While the call to 'do justice' must always be to the forefront for a people who are following Christ, we also 'do justice' in our very gathering and praying. This is done very clearly during the prayers of intercession. These prayers bring our problems and the problems of the world, before the community and before God. We remember our responsibility for our neighbour and for all peoples, and indeed for all of creation, when we pray our intercessory prayers. These prayers remind us that while we are presently enjoying a taste of heaven, while we are slowly being divinised, we are still here on earth and have earthly cares and responsibilities. These concerns are not foreign to God and so we can pray in confidence.

Live 'in accordance with the Lord's Day'
Saint Ignatius of Antioch (AD 50-115) summarises very beauti-fully the Eucharistic vocation of a Christian. It is to live 'in accordance with the Lord's Day', *iuxta dominicam viventes* (*Ad Magnes*, 9, 1. Cited in *Sacramentum Caritatis*, 72). The Lord's Day, the day on which we remember the resurrection, the day on which most Catholics gather to celebrate the Eucharist is to penetrate our whole lives. That which we do on Sunday is to influence that which we do every other day. The Eucharist is a call to live lives of thanksgiving, of truth, of justice. It is a call to live as Jesus lived, and to proclaim the Kingdom of God. The Eucharist schools us so that we can see the Kingdom of God in the many acts of kindness encountered each day, and empowers us with the Holy Spirit to proclaim the coming of the Kingdom of God when we shall join God for life eternal. The bread and wine, the Body and Blood of Christ, are a foretaste of the escha-tological feast, the banquet that we shall enjoy with God in heaven. The celebration of the Lord's Day, the first day of the week, and everyday Christian life are to interpenetrate one another. 'Living in accordance with the Lord's Day' means allowing that which we celebrate on the Sunday, or indeed the Eucharist we pray on any day of the week, to permeate our daily life. We are to live differently because we feed on the Body and the Blood of Christ. Jesus' words to his followers in Matthew's gospel, remain his words to us now – 'You yourselves, give them something to eat' (Mt 14:16). Each of us is truly called, together with Jesus, to be bread broken for the life of the world.

Notes

CHAPTER ONE

1. All Christians claim to follow Jesus Christ, but within the Christian tradition there are different ecclesial (Church) expressions of faith. Catholics are distinctive in affirming the Petrine ministry (papacy) as an integral element of the institutional Church. The principle of sacramentality is also central. Catholics understand God to be present and operative in history through the visible, the concrete. Christ is regarded as the sacrament of the encounter with God, the Church the sacrament of encounter with Christ and the sacraments as (seven) signs and means by which the encounter with Christ is made manifest and celebrated. Catholicism sees itself as a Church of the 'both/and' in its approach to things such as nature and grace, faith and reason, scripture and tradition.

2. The *Shema* is the central prayer for Jewish people. A declaration of faith in one God, the scripture passages prayed reaffirm the basic tenets of Jewish faith.

3. The *Didache*, known in English as 'The Teaching of the Apostles', is a piece of writing from the early days of the Church. It was probably written in the early part of the second century, and it provides very interesting information on early Church practices and teachings. The *Didache* can be easily accessed on the internet.

4. The Fiftieth International Eucharistic Congress, held in Dublin in 2012, took as its theme the very rich notion of 'communion'. For more on the multi-faceted nature of this term see *The Eucharist: Communion with Christ and with one another* (Dublin: Veritas, 2011), nn.7-19.

5. The Second Vatican Council was held in Rome from 1962 to 1965. The first document to be promulgated by the Council was concerned with the liturgy, and began with the words, *Sacrosanctum Concilium*, which means 'this sacred council' (1963).

6. This quote is taken from the *Summa Theologiae* of St Thomas Aquinas, the work for which he is most famous.

CHAPTER TWO

1. *Lumen Gentium* is the Latin title for one of the principle teaching documents of the Second Vatican Council. As is customary with important Church documents it is known by its opening words - *Lumen Gentium*, the Latin for 'light of the nations'. In its English translation the document begins 'Christ is the Light of nations'.

2. See chapter five for more on the meal practice of Jesus.

3. For further information on the development of the ministry of leadership in the early Church see Francis A. Sullivan, *From Apostles to Bishops: The Development of the Episcopacy in the Early Church* (New York: The Newman Press, 2001).

4. Gary Macy, *The Banquet's Wisdom: A Short History of the Theologies of the Lord's Supper* (New York: The Paulist Press, 1992), 22.

5. The preaching of people such as John Chrysostom (c.347-407) stressed the necessity of purity of conscience before receiving. However it seems that infrequent reception was already long established by this time. For an interesting scholarly discussion of this topic see Paul F. Bradshaw, *Reconstructing Early Christian Worship.* (London: SPCK, 2009), 28-37.

6. There are still various rites in use in the Catholic Church. See the *Catechism of the Catholic Church*, n. 1203.

CHAPTER THREE

1. Paul VI speaks insightfully regarding this mystery in his General Audience, Live the Paschal Mystery. Published in *L'Osservatore Romano*, the newspaper of the Holy See, 17 April 1969.

2. Louis Bouyer of the Oratory, *Eucharist: Theology and Spirituality of the Eucharistic Prayer*. Translated by Charles U. Quinn (Notre Dame/ London: University of Notre Dame Press, 1968), 84-85.

3. *The Eucharist: Communion with Christ and with one another* (Dublin: Veritas, 2011), n. 97.

4. Charles Péguy, *Portal of the Mystery of Hope* (London/New York: Continuum, 1996), 60. *Le porche du mystère de la deuxième*, Paris, 1929.

5. Aquinas is clear, the Eucharist has the power to forgive all sin, however the recipient may not be open to receive this forgiveness: 'Now whoever is conscious of mortal sin, has within him an obstacle to receiving the effect of this sacrament; since he is not a proper recipient of this sacrament, both because he is not alive spiritually, and so he ought not to eat the spiritual nourishment, since nourishment is confined to the living; and because he cannot be united with Christ, which is the effect of this sacrament, as long as he retains an attachment towards mortal sin' (*ST* III q.79 , a. 3 c).

6. *The Catechism of the Catholic Church* teaches that mortal sin 'is a radical possibility of human freedom' (n.1861). Three conditions are necessary for a sin to be deemed mortal – grave matter, full knowledge and deliberate consent. The conversion of heart necessitated for a person to turn

back to God from mortal sin is 'normally accomplished within the setting of the sacrament of Reconciliation' (*Catechism*, n. 1856).

7. The *General Instruction of the Roman Missal* provides guidance for the Church so that we might worthily celebrate the Mass.

8. See also Leviticus 20:26: 'You shall be holy to me; for I the Lord am holy, and I have separated you from the other peoples to be mine.'

9. The Bible is the book of the Church, God's special revelation to us. The Church, the People of God, under the guidance of the Holy Spirit discerned the books deemed to have been inspired by God to include in the biblical canon. Catholic and Protestant Christians agree on the same canon of the New Testament, twenty-seven books. Catholics accept a longer Old Testament canon of forty-six books while Protestants decided on a shorter canon of thirty-nine books.

10. The Divine Office (Liturgy of the Hours) is a very rich prayer resource of the Christian Church. It provides psalms and readings for regular prayer during the day. It has existed from the earliest times, to fulfil the Lord's command to pray without ceasing. 'The Office is … the prayer not only of the clergy but of the whole People of God.' *Canticum Laudis*. Apostolic Constitution promulgating the revised book of the *Liturgy of the Hours*, Pope Paul VI, November 1, 1970.

11. The word *metanoia* is a Greek term which speaks of a person's change of mind, a change of heart. When used in the Gospels it refers to an interior transformation, revealed in a transformed way of life; in other words, a conversion.

12. Nicholas Lash, *Believing Three Ways in One God* (London: SCM Classics 2002), 8.

CHAPTER FOUR

1. The word *epiclesis* is used to describe the way we, the Church, call upon the power of the Holy Spirit to consecrate the gifts, that is, to change the Bread and Wine into Christ's Body and Blood.

2. 'The Church celebrates the sacraments as a priestly community structured by the baptismal priesthood and the priesthood of ordained ministers' *Catechism of the Catholic Church*, n. 1132.

3. Nicholas Lash, *Believing Three Ways in One God* (London: SCM Press, 1992), 1.

4. *Summa Theologiae* II-II q.83 a. 9 c.

5. St Teresa of Avila, *Spiritual Masters: The Way of Perfection.* Translated by E. Allison Peers. (London: Sheed and Ward, 1977), 183. For St Thomas Aquinas on the Our Father see Paul Murray, *Praying with Confidence: Aquinas on the Lord's Prayer* (London: Continuum, 2010).

6. CANON VI. – 'If any one saith, that the sacraments of the New Law do not contain the grace which they signify; or, that they do not confer that grace on those who do not place an obstacle thereunto; as though they were merely outward signs of grace or justice received through faith, and certain marks of the Christian profession, whereby believers are distinguished amongst people from unbelievers; let him be anathema.' The Second Vatican Council reiterates this important teaching in positive language. For 'well-disposed members of the faithful, the liturgy of the sacraments and sacramentals sanctifies almost every event in their lives; they are given access to the stream of divine grace which flows from the paschal mystery of the passion, death, the resurrection of Christ, the font from which all sacraments and sacramentals draw their power' (*Sacrosanctum Concilium* n. 61).

7. The words of Brendan Kennelly in his poem 'Begin', give clear expression to what Eucharist calls us to: 'Though we live in a world that dreams of ending/that always seems about to give in/something that will not acknowledge conclusion/insists that we forever begin.'

8. The words of St Thomas Aquinas succinctly explain why there is a belief that communion should be received on the tongue: 'Out of reverence towards this sacrament [the Holy Eucharist], nothing touches it, but what is consecrated; hence the corporal and the chalice are consecrated, and likewise the priest's hands, for touching this sacrament.' (*Summa Theologiae* III, q. 82, a. 3, ad. 8). *Memoriale Domini*, the *Instruction on the Manner of Administering Holy Communion* issued by The Congregation for Divine Worship in 1969 also addressed this issue, and presented communion on the tongue as preferable as it ensured more reverence for the consecrated species. The challenge to us all is to receive with reverence, whether on our tongue or in our hands.

9. *General Instruction on the Roman Missal*, n. 281.

CHAPTER FIVE

1. See *Catechism of the Catholic Church*, II.1244

2. For an informed and compassionate reading of the Churches teaching in this complex area see *The Eucharist: Communion with Christ and with one another* (Dublin: Veritas, 2011), nn. 24-32. The section entitled 'A Eucharistic Congress for All' insightfully notes that 'Everyone can contribute to reform in the Church' (n. 32).

3. In the early days of the Christian Church the initiatory rite seems to have consisted of an anointing with oil followed by immersion in water 'in the name of the Father, and of the Son, and of the Holy Spirit'. Admission to Eucharist followed immediately. The Orthodox and Oriental Churches still follow this practice.

4. This boycott was the result of the decision of Sheila Cloney (Protestant), married to Sean Cloney (Catholic), not to send their daughters to a Catholic school, despite the local priest's insistence that she be bound by a signed pre-marriage agreement to bring up any children as Catholic (depicted in the film *A Love Divided*, 1999).

5. The first Ecumenical Directory was published in two parts, one in 1967 and the other in 1970. A revised edition was published in 1993.

6. *On admitting other Christians to Eucharistic communion in the Catholic Church* mainly repeats earlier teaching, with some interesting changes in language. *The Code of Canon Law*, issued in 1983, bases its code (canon 844.4) on the 1967 *Directory*, requesting that a person spontaneously ask for the sacrament, demonstrate Catholic faith in respect of the sacraments and be properly disposed.

7. *Directory for the Application of Principles and Norms on Ecumenism* (London: CTS, 1993), [Pontifical Council for Promoting Christian Unity].

8. *The Catechism of the Catholic Church* teaches that the Eucharist is 'properly the sacrament of those in full communion with the Church' (n. 1395).

9. *One Bread, One Body*. A teaching document on the Eucharist in the life of the Church, and the establishment of general norms on sacramental sharing. Catholic Bishops' Conferences of England and Wales, Ireland and Scotland, 1998.

10. 'One Bread, One Body ... One Year', A response by Bishop Richard Clarke one year on. First published in the Winter edition of *Search*. http://www.ireland.anglican.org/information/86. Accessed 4 February 2012.

11. Don Camillo is a character created by the Italian writer and journalist Giovannino Guareschi (1908-1968), based on a real figure, a priest who had been imprisoned in concentration camps. Camillo, and his co-protagonist, Peppone, the communist mayor, live in a small town in rural Italy just after the Second World War. The stories were first published in a weekly magazine and later in eight books. They were subsequently made into films (1952 and 1965).

CHAPTER SIX

1. Paul F. Bradshaw, *Reconstructing Early Christian Worship*, (London: SPCK, 2009), 28-35.

2. Christology is the name given to the part of theology that deals specifically with Jesus Christ. A 'high' Christology emphasises the divinity of Christ, a 'low' Christology the humanity. Some contemporary

Christologies are so 'low' that Jesus is presented solely as a human, and the question of his divinity only arises in its outright rejection. This development is essentially a rejection of Christian belief in a Trinitarian God.

3. One side of the debate presented Christ's presence in realistic and physical terms, Paschasius Radbertus (c.785-c.860) was prominent here. In response others, such as Ratramnus of Corbie (died c. 868) adopted a more symbolic and spiritualised interpretation.

4. Miri Rubin, *Corpus Christi: The Eucharist in Late Medieval Culture* (Cambridge: Cambridge University Press, 1991), 148.

5. Elevation of the chalice was the subject of much discussion as there was a fear that elevation might lead to spillage of the consecrated wine. Also, the fact that one could not 'see' the wine meant there was less popular pressure for this to happen.

6. Rubin, *Corpus Christi*, 58.

7. The requirement to fast from midnight the night before, added to a growing sense of unworthiness, did not encourage regular communion. From today's perspective it is remarkable to note that at the final Mass of the Eucharistic Congress held in Ireland in 1932 it is probable that only one person, the celebrant, Archbishop Michael J. Curley of Baltimore, would have communicated. The majority of people would have received at earlier Masses held that day. This was normal practice at a high Mass, and spoke of a very different vision of Church to the vision which began to emerge later in the twentieth century.

8. It is interesting to note that many of our Anglican sisters and brothers have a Eucharistic faith similar to ours. They reserve the Blessed Sacrament in tabernacles, celebrate Benediction, and some congregations have exposition of the Blessed Sacrament.

9. Juliana served at the leper-hospital attached to the Premonstratensian house of Mont Cornillon in Liège. See Rubin, *Corpus Christi*, 169 ff.

10. *Vita Julianae II*, chapter 2, n. 6. Authorship unknown.

11. *Vita Julianae II*, chapter 2, n. 6.

12. The Divine Office, or the Liturgy of the Hours, is recited at various times during the day by religious and by some lay people. It consists of psalms and other readings from the Bible. Feast days will have special prayers and hymns, and some of the Catholic Churches most famous traditional Eucharistic hymns were composed by St Thomas Aquinas for the Office of Corpus Christi.

13. Saint Peter-Julian Eymard was the founder of the Congregation of the Blessed Sacrament.

CHAPTER SEVEN

1. *Fides et Ratio, Encyclical Letter on the Relationship between Faith and Reason*, 1998.

2. 'This is not a formal, but a substantial conversion; nor is it a kind of natural movement: but, with a name of its own, it can be called "transubstantiation"' (*Summa Theologiae III* q.75 a.4 c). He adapted his understanding of this word from Aristotelian philosophy.

3. 'St Thomas uses Aristotle's language, but it breaks down in speaking of the Eucharist. It does not break down because there is some more accurate language in which the whole thing can be explained. It breaks down because it is language. We are dealing here with something that transcends our concepts and can only be spoken of by stretching language to breaking point: we are dealing here with mystery,' Herbert McCabe, 'Eucharistic Change' in *Priests and People* (1994) 9: 217-221.

4. 'By the consecration of the bread and of the wine, a conversion is made of the whole substance of the bread into the substance of the body of Christ our Lord, and of the whole substance of the wine into the substance of His blood; which conversion is, by the holy Catholic Church, suitably and properly called Transubstantiation' (*Thirteenth Session*, chapter four).

5. 'The mode of Christ's presence under the Eucharistic species is unique. It raises the Eucharist above all the sacraments as "the perfection of the spiritual life and the end to which all the sacraments tend." In the most blessed sacrament of the Eucharist "the body and blood, together with the soul and divinity, of our Lord Jesus Christ and, therefore, the whole Christ is truly, really, and substantially contained." "This presence is called 'real' – by which is not intended to exclude the other types of presence as if they could not be 'real' too, but because it is presence in the fullest sense: that is to say, it is a substantial presence by which Christ, God and human, makes himself wholly and entirely present."' *Catechism of the Catholic Church*, n. 1374.

6. 'In the *epiclesis*, the Church asks the Father to send his Holy Spirit (or the power of his blessing) on the bread and wine, so that by his power they may become the body and blood of Jesus Christ and so that those who take part in the Eucharist may be one body and one spirit.' *Catechism of the Catholic Church*, n. 1353.

7. Cardinal Kasper wrote this in a paper given at an ecumenical conference. It is published in *Holy Spirit, The Church, And Christian Unity: Proceedings Of The Consultation Held At The Monastery Of Bose, Italy, 14-20 October, 2002* (Bibliotheca Ephemeridum Theologicarum Lovaniensium).

8. Herbert McCabe, 'Priesthood' in *God, Christ and Us*. Edited by Brian Davies (London/New York: Continuum, 2003), 151-155:151. Passages of Scripture, such as those dealing with the 'wrath of God', also need to be taken into account as we continually strive, as Church, to develop the most truthful understanding of God available to us during our earthly existence.

9. Herbert McCabe, 'Priesthood', 155.

10. 'Jesus atoned for our faults and made satisfaction for our sins to the Father' (*Catechism of the Catholic Church*, 615). Over the centuries theologians have developed different theories to try to explain better the redemptive nature of Christ's passion and death in God's plan of salvation. St Thomas Aquinas explores this question of how our sins are forgiven through the power of Christ's passion in *Summa Theologiae III* q.49 a.1.

11. See Herbert McCabe, 'Washing and Eucharist' in *God, Christ and Us* (London: Continuum, 2003), 83-87.

CHAPTER EIGHT

1. Nicholas Wolterstorff, 'Justice as a Condition of Authentic Liturgy', *Theology Today* (1991), 48:6-21.

2. 'He has told you, O mortal, what is good; and what does the Lord require of you but to do justice, and to love kindness, and to walk humbly with your God?' (Micah 6:8).

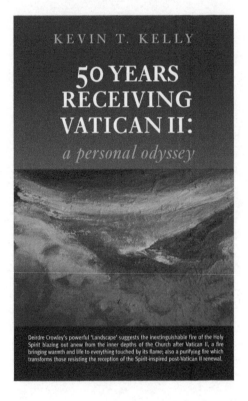

Also Available from Columba

Reaping the Harvest: Fifty Years after Vatican II

Edited by Suzanne Mulligan

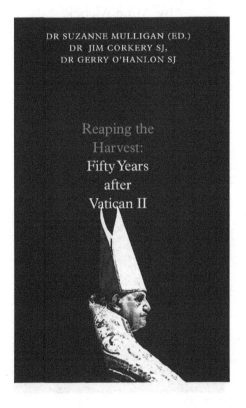

Suzanne Mulligan, Jim Corkery SJ and Gerry O'Hanlon SJ examine the implications of the Second Vatican Council at the time, and the continued importance of the teachings today, through a critique of some of the Council's major documents.

the columba press

<u>Also Available from Columba</u>

*Text and Tips for Spiritual Directors
and for Personal Prayer*

by Anne Alcock

This revised edition of *Text and Tips* features new additions
alongside classic selections from the original publication, which
proved so popular.

the columba press